BLIND

A MEMOIR

Belo Miguel Cipriani

Blind: A Memoir

Published by Wheatmark®
610 East Delano Street, Suite 104
Tucson, Arizona 85705 U.S.A.
www.wheatmark.com

ISBN: 978-1-60494-555-3 (paperback)
ISBN: 978-1-60494-630-7 (Kindle)
LCCN: 2011928117

Disclaimer

This memoir is based on my experience in losing my vision and learning to navigate the sighted-centric world. The blind are, before anything else, people and therefore may respond to or encounter different experiences with adaptive technology and social services from the ones described in this book. My memoir has in part actual events, persons, and companies. However, a number of the characters, incidents, and companies portrayed and the names used herein are fictionalized. Any resemblance of the fictitious incidents, companies, or characters to actual events, companies, or persons, living or dead, is entirely coincidental.

I dedicate *Blind: A Memoir* to my mom, Sonia, my four sisters, Emely, Rocio, Dulce, and Michelle, and my brother in-law, John. They were my backbone through my emotional and physical recovery. Without their support, I would have not been able to conquer blindness.

Contents

Acknowledgments

I want to thank Kate, Tori, Sarah, Lauren, Chelsa, Jeramy, Richard, and Adam. They are all members of my writing posse whose feedback helped shape my memoir.

I also want to express my deep appreciation to LeShawn, Jeff, Maurice, Don, Tammie, Whinde, Mona, Hilary, and Marisa. The group of friends that never stopped dialing my cell phone, even when I stopped returning calls for a while.

A special thanks to Justin T. Lotspeich, Darth Cabrol-Easton, and Brad Paterson, who never allowed me to give up on publishing and were great cheerleaders/coaches throughout my entire manuscript editing process.

Introduction

For two years, I struggled with the idea of putting my story on paper. Although I received plenty of encouragement, I had a pain in my stomach when I tried to write it down that told me it was not time yet. I now know there were two powerful forces keeping me from doing what I understood would be beneficial for both my mind and my soul. The first notion holding me back was the hope that I could possibly get my sight back. It was obvious to me later that denial was the toughest phase to surpass in my mourning period. Second, I was afraid that putting myself back in all of those moments of pain, sorrow, and anxiety would spiral me into depression. I locked away any thoughts of telling my story.

After my first writing class, I was inspired by all the kind voices in the room that applauded my initial in-class writing exercise. I went back to my dorm, still feeling uneasy about writing my story, and attempted to write "The Siren Song." Three hours of listening to my computer read back the words and sentences that captured my horrific fate tortured me. For a few minutes, I contemplated dropping out of the class altogether. I heard Madge grunt during my moment of despair and confusion. I felt her front paws on my leg and kept my hands on the keyboard. She began to lick my tears and got me to smile. I decided to put "The Siren Song" on ice and dedicated my first piece, "Hi Dad," to my new partner, who gave me the best pep talk ever.

After submitting my first piece to class for workshopping, I focused on side stories and gathered the skills and tools needed to take on the more emotional chapters, which came toward the later part of my master's program. Especially in the beginning, I found myself using humor and self-deprecation to make the difficult passages easier. As I progressed through the graduate course work, I gathered the strength to attempt the more painful and numbing parts of my memoir, only working on the stories my soul would tolerate at the time.

When I was newly blind, my friends and family struggled to find any memoirs about adults losing sight to read to me. By writing a story that reflects a more contemporary journey through blindness, I want to offer hope to the future generations of blind men and women who seek understanding and empathy.

1

The Siren's Song

One of the first sounds I learned to detect and fully understand was the song of a screaming ambulance. As a little boy, I would run toward the window every time that scary noise appeared in my simple world. I would glance back at my mom, my hand flat on the glass, and eagerly await a response. Mom would sadly answer, "Someone's hurt; we should close our eyes and pray for them." As I got older, I realized these massive sound waves didn't just alert one of another's injury, but, in many cases, they shouted that death was nearby and lingering. As I journeyed through different parts of the world, I was quite intrigued to notice that despite the language spoken, that high-pitched tune had the same meaning in every quaint, small town and every grand metropolis.

Working in San Francisco's financial district desensitized me, and I could tuck away all of my childhood fears and superstitions. Those chaotic alarms that came from the fast-moving white vans and cop cars became part of my daily soundtrack. On a fogless and busy Friday filled with errands, I dared to take on the condensed shops and piles of people on the sloped streets of downtown San Francisco. An overpriced haircut and two cups of coffee later, my over-caffeinated

1

body vibrated down a quiet set of steps near Market Street to make some calls. I had only been single for a short period; however, with the help of close friends and the Internet, I had quickly added a few names to my trendy new phone. After sliding my thumb up and down the silver buttons a couple of times, I was able to schedule a dinner for later that day with an old lover the Web had reconnected me with. I remained on the steps, enjoying the intoxicating high one gets from scheduling that special date. I stared as if in a trance into the hazel sky and began to drift. Beethoven's Fifth started to play. I had assigned new ringtones to friends and family since the addition of my slick, hip toy and didn't always recognize the tone. I read the three-letter word and quickly answered, "Hi, Mom."

She started to tell me about her trip as I uncoiled my Armani tie with my free hand and stretched my right leg. It was our usual weekly check-in until she cautiously said, "I hope you're not going out tonight. It's the thirteenth, you know!"

I smiled and replied, "I'm not planning to stay out that late." Just like when I told lies as a kid, I looked away from the phone as if the lens on the camera were an extension of her stare. Suddenly, I felt and saw a roaring fire truck make its way down Second Street and turn onto Market. Knowing well the fire department was the opening act, I said to my mom, "It's too loud; let me call you tomorrow." The concert was in full session by the time I closed my phone and snuggled it back in my pants pocket. I rushed down to the subway to get away, my mother's words guiding me back to my adolescence.

Although I have four sisters, I always felt my mom was more overprotective of me, since I was a gay man living in a Latino neighborhood with old worldviews. As a teen, Mom would always warn me to be careful, even if I was just going across the street. She told me of distant relatives and friends who shared my "likes" and how they often disappeared, leaving nothing but memories behind. Like Xavier's School for the Gifted, my mom would let my friends hide in our home where they felt safe, accepted, and, most importantly, not like mutants. Most of the people I was bringing home were other teenage boys I met on the newly introduced World Wide Web. Unlike me, they lacked their parents' support and often just wanted to hang out. My mom kept all gatherings PG-13, and everyone felt comfortable with the relaxed social agenda.

Among the flock of new acquaintances were two brothers—both gay and almost a decade apart in age. Although the elder brother was obviously the more responsible and ethical one, the younger brother seemed to call the shots.

Carlos, although only sixteen, was as experienced as the guys my older sisters dated. He drank, smoked, and mysteriously attended high school in another city. Carlos was a legend within the local gay community. He was often courted by men twice his age and always managed to get out of relationships before they got serious. His older brother, Rodrigo, was the complete opposite: he would rarely talk and was socially awkward. Nonetheless, the brothers and I, and a fourth guy named Jesus, became inseparable for a while. Armed with our fake IDs and Rodrigo as our reliable driver, we ventured to gay bars as far north from our San Jose neighborhood as Sacramento and as far south as Salinas. It was both fun and extremely deviant to be part of the crowd of kids who were popular outside of school cliques. This is how I rationalized the concept of staying up late and drinking on school nights, allowing myself to get caught up in the toxic gay scene of the time.

We had been hanging out for a few months and could have printed tour-style T-shirts with all the clubs we had visited. It was a typical Friday night, and we were making our way to the notorious Bench and Bar club in Oakland when I sobered up the car by saying, "Umm, I can't hang out next weekend."

Jesus nearly spilled his Irish slurpie and asked, "Why, bitch?"

I shyly replied, "I have to take my SATs; I want to go to college."

Their disengaged and uninterested sighs filled the car. After that, things were never the same. I repeatedly canceled on them as I prepared for college and, eventually, was admitted to a small Catholic university in Belmont, California, where my life took a new turn. Carlos and the gang came to my dorm a few times but never stayed for very long. We maintained a loose friendship for a while, but as years passed, they became just other faces in a bar I would fondly greet after slow recognition.

Rejecting my mother's admonition to respect the power of the day, I happily prepared for a night on the town. Pete and I had been flirting for years, and although this was not a first date, it felt like such. We agreed to meet at "corporate headquarters," Castro and Eighteenth Street, where we then veered to the latest gay hangout. My friend Don called, and I struggled to make out his words over the background music at The Café, a few blocks down. Pete and I then agreed to move the party because he was eager to meet my friends.

After a few introductions and exchange of hugs, I realized

I had left my jacket at the last place. I excused myself and made my way back to Badlands. I picked up my coat and decided to wear it despite the warm air. I was halfway back to The Café when I heard a childlike voice say, "Hey, Belo!"

I turned my head toward the right and saw Rodrigo leaning on a wall that curved into a parking lot. I walked toward him and quickly embraced his thin body. I anxiously asked, "How's Carlos?"

He responded, "He's over here; come quick."

I smiled, following him toward the back of the building. I saw Carlos and two others I did not know leaning against a dark-colored SUV, and I nonchalantly walked up and asked, "Hey, Carlos; what's up?"

He rolled his eyes and said, "I'm surprised you're out and not taking a class."

Puzzled, I answered, "What the hell does that mean?"

Rodrigo, who usually didn't say much, then echoed Carlos, saying, "Yeah, we've seen you change; you think you're the shit now."

Carlos then walked toward me saying, "You know, I own a real estate company and am making a bunch of money. We make more money than you'll ever see!"

His dark brown eyes looked straight into mine as he pushed me back. Tapping into my martial arts training, I allowed my body to absorb the push and took three steps back.

I looked around as if I were taking pictures with my eyes and said, "Good for you!" I began to shift my body and turn around and felt the first impact in the back of my head. A cyclone of punches then followed, and I was knocked to the ground. A series of kicking and kneeing came after, and I tried hard to block what I could until my body surrendered. I felt warm liquid roll down my head and face, and I looked up for a quick moment and saw Carlos kick his leg back as he charged his foot into my face. I yelled, "Carlos, nooo!" and before I completed pronouncing the o-o-o, I felt his boot crushing my right eye.

I began to experience the deepest silence in my life. New to darkness, I was unsure if I was alive or not. I dug into my pocket and pulled out my phone. I hit the "send" key twice and heard Don's voice. I then whispered, "Help." I lay flat on the pavement feeling only the warm liquid wrapping my head, my broken skin kissing the concrete. I felt like a sailor in a vast black sea, falling under the spell of the familiar song, the hypnotic sound growing louder and louder as the choir of sirens called for me.

2

Raffle Day

I was in Mrs. Del Mar's second-grade class when I had my first encounter with vision loss. It was a typical weekday full of math and science activities with a quick story time sandwiched before lunch. I don't recall the book Mrs. Del Mar was reading to us; the only thing that plays vividly in my mind is sitting on the floor, legs tucked against my Ninja Turtle shirt. My eyes completely glazed in awe and admiration for the beautiful woman who read so clearly to us. The story came to an end, and then she went on to make a few announcements: "Today, I'll be handing out tickets for this Friday's raffle after we all get our eyes checked by the school nurse this afternoon." The bell rang, and she then enthusiastically yelled, "See you guys after lunch!"

Every week Mrs. Del Mar would add the name of a student who showed excellence in answering questions in class or for good behavior into a yellow plastic container that lived on her desk. Although getting tickets was never an issue for me, it was a few months into the year, and I had yet to hear my name called out. I would sometimes lie in bed, after my mom or dad had tucked me in, and dream about winning one of those great prizes the other kids had taken home. Although none of the toys or school supplies the students won had much monetary value, I still wanted to be part of that handful of boys and girls that were cheered and clapped for during the gift selection process each week.

The bell rang, and I quickly shoved a chicken nugget in my mouth and rushed my tray to a small window where a nice woman took it from me. I ran as fast as my little Reeboks would get me back to my class. I was the last one in, and Mrs. Del Mar said, "You're late again; the nurse is already waiting for you in her office."

I joined three of my classmates at the nurse's office, the same classmates near me in line every time they used the alphabet to herd us. The nurse signaled me in with a quick hand gesture, and I immediately jumped up. She had me look into a tube and read a series of lines. I did fine until reaching the bottom two rows. I then started to rub my eyes, and the nurse kindly said, "Don't do that, hon; that doesn't help." She quickly scribbled on a paper and asked me to give it to my mom.

A school bus ride later, I made my way home and ripped my backpack in half and handed my mom the note from the nurse. Unable to understand the English, she had my older sister translate it for her. My mother then asked my sister to book an appointment with the optometrist at the mall for the next day. I was excited to miss school because that meant I would not have to be there until Raffle Day.

My dad wore glasses, and I thought it was somewhat cool to get a pair of my own. I showed up to school with my new set of eyes and spotted another girl with a new pair of spectacles too. No one in class mentioned my glasses, and class work resumed as usual. A few minutes before the day was done, Mrs. Del Mar struck a triangle to announce the big weekly raffle. My eyes, now magnified by the glass in front of them, glowed with joy. Mrs. Del Mar reached into the yellow shiny box and said, "We're only choosing one winner today, since we're short on time." She then paused and called my name flatly. I couldn't believe it! My new glasses were already proving to be good luck for me. I hopped to the front of the class and was overwhelmed by the voices cheering and shouting. Mrs. Del Mar then pulled out a giant black plastic bag, the ones I'm sure they used in the school kitchen. She went on to say, "Since it's just you this week, let's change things around a bit." I ran my fingers on the side of my hair and behind my neck and remained silent. Mrs. Del Mar continued, "There are a few prizes in this bag, and you must stick your hand in and pick one without peeking."

I quietly asked, "Why can't I just look in the bag and pick something?"

Mrs. Del Mar replied, "Well, because someday you may not have your sight." I did as I was told, not fully understanding her words, and pulled out a box of scented markers. Grinning from ear to ear, I made my way back to my desk.

3

Decay

It had only been two days since my betrayers banished me to another dimension. Nothing felt, smelled, tasted, or, to my surprise, sounded the same. Taking a few steps was torturous; moving through space without sight seemed like an out-of-body experience. My coworker Josie drove me to the hospital for the first scheduled surgery as I had no close relatives in the city. Josie worked out of our Placerville office, which is a two-hour drive from San Francisco. I had only been with the firm for about a month; however, Josie and I quickly became friends as our roles permitted us to talk on the phone daily. She was among the group who came to offer me their support during the first forty-eight hours following the assault. Josie was the first person I met without sight. I had a visual memory for everyone else, but we had only known each other through phone and email interaction. She practiced yoga and was always taking some sculpting or painting class after work. What Josie lacked in size, she made up for in strength. As she helped my sore and bruised body climb into her car, I felt the safety of her fit arms. Her calm voice helped me not focus on the excruciating pain I had been experiencing for hours and allowed me to reflect on my fate. I focused on the endless rollercoaster ride of San Francisco hills, feeling lost in this very familiar landscape.

"We're almost there; we're just hitting some light traffic," Josie said.

I struggled to respond, "Thank you, Josie; thank you very much," still surprised she had offered to help after only knowing me a few weeks.

"Glad I could be here today," she quickly answered.

One of my mom's old sayings popped into my head, and I repeated it: "They say that one can discover who his true friends are when he's in jail or the hospital."

Josie answered, "I believe that."

I was admitted quickly and rushed to an operating room. Josie and I said our goodbyes, and I felt like I was being prepared to embark on a voyage. I heard both male and female voices prance around me as someone pasted stickers on my chest and another hooked cords to them. I then felt a third person on the other side of the bed unfolding a warm towel as I was noticeably shivering. A kind voice then said, "Mr. Cipriani, we'll be starting in a few minutes."

I sighed as I waited for the anesthesia to make its way through my worn limbs. I slowly faded into a deeper darkness, mentally asking Carlos, *How could you?*

The next few days were extremely confusing and physically painful. I don't remember leaving the hospital and thought I was dreaming when I woke up to my mother touching my face.

I smelled her lavender perfume and asked, "Mom, is that you?"

She replied, "Yes, I've been here since yesterday." I felt myself embraced by her calm aura.

I whispered, "I'm sorry; I'm sorry about it all."

She answered with her usual serene style, "Shh, it's going to get all better soon."

The doctors struggled to get me on a painkiller that I could stomach. I spent two days throwing up Vicodin and another two days purging Percocet. It got to the point where I threw up my own feces; it made me so angry to lose control of my body and slowly watch it rot. The ophthalmologist did not want me to bathe, since he was afraid water would get into my eyes and cause an infection. Despite my mom's effort to clean my face, every time she administered the eye drops, the overgrown stubble and scabs would irritate me as the sweat from the bandages made me feel like I was withering away in a dark hole where things went to die.

In between my naps, I reflected on my last relationship—Jim—and the three years as close friends and the four as lovers. I gave in to my desire to call and tell him what happened. I suppose I was hoping there was still enough love between us for him to want to be there. I was hopeful and banking on the genuine human compassion I had discovered in friends like Josie. I asked my mom to help me dial his number, and tears began to crowd my face when I heard his voice. He had a tough time understanding my sentences, but said he would be over later.

It seemed to be immediately that my mom announced his arrival, and I nodded to signal her it was okay to let him in the room.

"Shit!" Jim gasped as I heard his steps approach our old bed. "Are they in jail yet?" he asked.

I answered, "No, I talked to a Detective Robins yesterday though. They'll be starting an investigation. Can I get a hug?" I asked shyly.

"I'm not sure that's a good idea. Umm, you look really fragile, and I don't want to *inconvenience* you."

I said, "Okay." His odd choice of words was ricocheting in the stale room.

He added, "I do want to help though; what can I do?"

I asked if he could move some money around for me, since my mom's English was limited, and she had been out of the country long enough to be unfamiliar and uneasy with my modern ways of banking. He took the stack of papers and patted me on the shoulder, saying, "I'll take care of it."

The next day my mom asked, "When will Jim be arriving?"

I responded, "Soon, very soon, he promised."

I refused to count the days, but I had the sinking feeling that here was another person I had trusted who kicked me when I was down. Every day became more melancholy for me as the number of unanswered voicemails grew.

After one session of eye drops, my mom said, "That money is gone, but it's not for us to judge." I felt her tears fall and mine creeping from under the bandages to join them. I prepared myself to sleep, feeling like unwanted Christmas trees left on curbs across America to decay.

4

Stone Pillows

Ilaunched out of my sleep after feeling the sensation that someone was climbing on top of me and pushing down on my chest, keeping me from breathing. I yelled Jim's name and suddenly realized I was standing on my bed, my head nearly touching the ceiling, in marionette form. I collapsed back onto my mattress and slowly started to chuckle as I said aloud, "What the fuck." I looked toward my left and saw my cat sleeping contentedly, completely unaware of my nightmare. I began to shift my body toward the other side of the canopy bed and forced myself to peer into the terrifying vacancy. I leaned over and caressed the pillow with my right hand where, for years, his head had nestled next to mine. I felt my tear ducts fill and jumped out of bed, using my fingers to push the salty mist back.

In a trance, my feet traced their nightly path to my study, avoiding eye contact with all the pieces of furniture that had witnessed not only his love, but also his infidelity and his sequences of lies. I reached my desk and quickly hit the computer's power button. I swiveled in my chair as I polished a pair of five-dollar reading glasses I got from Walgreens because I didn't feel like dealing with my contacts. I then typed the words "sleep" and "nightmare" and began to browse the numerous domains that answered my query. A mouse-clicking marathon later, I came across two sites and joined as a premium member. One website was focused on a diet of foods that promoted better sleep and rest. The second site provided a daily newsletter with tips on a variety of relaxation techniques that would result in a healthier sleeping pattern. All these Web pages relinquished data I desperately sought. Most importantly, I was proud of the fact that I found these solutions, proving to myself I was managing just fine on my own.

The next day at work I did my best to stay up and listen to a manager ramble about new website features. Unaware of the words creeping out of my mouth, I asked, "Um, why are we adding all these again?"

The manager smirked and said, "Well, because we must make our technology accessible to people with disabilities."

Uninterested, I responded, "Gotcha."

A few minutes later, I dragged my feet back to my lonely cubicle. I had been working at the bank for a few months now and hadn't made any friends yet, which was out of character for me. I kept my gaze on my blank notepad and avoided eye contact at all times. I feared that they somehow knew what had happened with my ex or worse that I would accidentally tell them in passing. I played the different scenarios in my head, anxious that I would blurt out, "Jim cheated again!" instead of saying, "Have a good one; see you tomorrow."

I returned to reviewing résumés for a position for which I was currently recruiting. Out of the thirty-something cover letters I perused, there were two Jims, and I fell off my chair each time the name appeared on my screen. Each time, I would squint at the little word, saying to myself, "I wonder if you're a cheater too." I minimized the CVs and double-clicked on my Web browser. I proceeded to type the words

"No cheating" and "dating." I found a site that offered free advice on where to meet monogamous singles and how to spot a cheater. I quickly initiated the three-step process by entering my email address in the edit field next to an image of a smiling heart. I finished typing my vitals and glanced at the bottom of the screen. Seeing the hour, I jumped up, grabbed my coat, and rushed to an early lunch.

I found a quiet coffee shop off an alley street and dialed my friend Eddie in L.A. He answered after the first ring and said, "Hi, Dollface! What's up?"

I replied, "Not so good. I can't sleep."

Eddie comforted me by saying, "Oh honey, you need to get online."

Rolling my eyes, I responded, "I already did; I joined this site that has these breathing techniques that can reduce my stress and help me sleep."

He giggled and said, "No, no, no. Do you have something to write with?"

I sighed and said, "Yup."

Eddie proceeded to give me a list of dating sites and told me about his great results with each one. I shrugged my shoulders, "Thanks, man, I'll check these out later. I got to get back to the office."

I called in sick the next day and spent the entire time tackling the list Eddie had provided for me. I booked a date for the weekend, since I was hoping to get better sleep before then.

Although the rest I was seeking never came, I decided to keep the date. We met at Orphan Andy's, a diner near my gym. The guy was striking and well-dressed; however, all I could think about was how to take his coat from him and roll it into a pillow to sleep on. His name was Marcelo, and he was new to San Francisco. He was full of stories and energy, which made me even more tired. I could see his frustration grow as I called him other names from my queue—first Ryan, then Tom. Halfway into his coffee, he clinched his teeth and said, "You know what? This is bull; I don't need this shit!" and stormed into the soggy street.

I wobbled out of the booth and into the drizzle, completely unconscious of my body's actions. I reached the sidewalk and screamed, "I'm sorry; I'm just tired!" My voice echoed off a few buildings, and the crowd standing outside the restaurant stopped talking to glance back at me with pity. It felt weird to get a pity party from bums holding damp cigarettes in their hands. I slumped back home, desperately trying to put the date behind me and arrived at a silent house that teased me with its Edwardian darkness.

Disoriented, I blindly stumbled through my living room and proceeded to dial my Internet company. I told them I was going on vacation and needed the service shut off for a few weeks. I am not sure why I made the call or why I lied, but I knew I had to log off for a while. I went back out to face the black rain and caught the bus to visit a busy bookstore where I browsed the cooking and self-help aisles. I spotted a small round table nestled next to a magazine rack and pulled up a chair to it. I fished out my PDA and began to type in a list of things I wanted to reintroduce in my life. I figured that if I wanted to move on, I had to gain back what I had lost during my relationship with Jim.

At the top of my list, I placed Capoeira and percussion classes, followed by cooking. The list went on, and when I got to item number ten, I clicked on the save option. I stared at the bottom of the miniature screen and began to study the date. I always believed in setting realistic goals for myself and came to the conclusion that two months was enough time to get the list going. April would be a great month, I thought to myself as I began to feel like my life was finally moving in a more positive direction. That night, for the first time in weeks, I fell into a deep sleep from which I did not wake until the cat's hungry call rang in my ears.

5

Gaymers

East San Jose, like many eastern sections of major California cities, is seen as the dangerous part of town. Despite its reputation for high levels of gang activity, drugs, and teen pregnancy, I felt safe and, most importantly, at home. So when my parents decided to upgrade, although we had only lived in this soulful neighborhood for a few months, I begged them to allow me to stay in the eastside school system. In this microcosm, no one teased me for being a vegetarian or cared that my mom spoke broken English. I was embraced for being myself, and acceptance was worth the hour bus ride from the lavish Rose Garden neighborhood every weekday.

Because I had opted to commute and not attend my local school and picked up dance and Capoeira, my father insisted I contribute to these costs by working part-time. Before I was old enough to get a work permit from my high school, I collected cans to sell to the recycling plant. Eventually, I was old enough to work at a salon as a receptionist where I made decent money for a teenager. Aside from good pay, I got free haircuts and was introduced to trends and fashion by the female stylists. Although I was confident in my appearance and could make even the most serious person crack a smile, I felt alone. I wanted the company of other gay boys to talk to about men and relationships. My search for other gays took me as far as joining the drama class, where I was grossly disappointed. To my surprise, all the guys were straight, and the one bi guy happened to be dating one of the prettiest girls at school.

My closest confidants were my four sisters whose ages ranged from nine to twenty-five and who varied in shades of skin, eyes, and hair. They all shared two traits: fiery tempers and great cheekbones. My sisters and I got along, yet I sometimes felt like an outsider to their sisterly bond. They shared clothes, makeup, and womanly advice. Disinterested with the female anatomy, I yearned for gay brothers.

My loneliness and my desire for gay friends made me quickly attach to them when I found them. The Lopez brothers—Carlos and Rodrigo—Jesus, and I instantly became friends. We shared the same sense of humor, taste in clothes, and enjoyed basking in the limelight. The first time we hung out came about rather casually. I had just gotten off of work at the salon and was listening to my pager's voicemail with my analog cell phone and sighed with boredom when I heard my different friends offering a night at the movies or at the arcades. I walked the two blocks from my job to my home, focusing on my unhappiness in the Rose Garden neighborhood. All the homes looked like they could be on the cover of a real-estate magazine with their manicured lawns and flowers. In my teenage trance of frustration, the blocks screamed homophobia, especially since all the homes pointed at the happiness of a straight marriage.

When I arrived home, my mother's petite frame was stretched over the stove, her red hair tightening in the steam coming from the stew pot. I gave her a kiss on the forehead and rushed to my room to check my email. I smiled when I saw I had a few messages from other gay guys, but my excitement melted away when I clicked each message and realized they were all from the East Coast. I walked away from the computer and started to change out of my work clothes. I whispered to myself, "I guess the movies it is."

I was removing the tags from my new Lacoste shirt when I heard the chime from an instant message. I ran toward my keyboard and noticed it was Jesus messaging me. We had talked in the San Jose chat room a few weeks ago but had yet to meet. He asked me what I was up to for the evening, and I was slightly embarrassed to admit my lame plans. He asked for my number, and, in a few seconds, we were talking on the phone, "Wanna hang out with us tonight?"

I responded, "Who is us?"

Jesus gave a bored sigh before answering, "Me, Carlos, and Rodrigo. I told them about you, and they want to meet you."

I asked shyly, "Are they a couple?"

Jesus laughed and said, "No, you silly, they are brothers." Immediately, I thought about how cool having a gay brother would be and agreed to go out.

"Can you come to our house?" Jesus continued saying, "We're off King Street." I smiled as I realized it was extremely close to my high school. "You are okay with coming to the east side, right?"

I told Jesus I went to school in the area and had no problem with it. I canceled on my friend for the movies and headed out of my room. I saw my mom and youngest sister asleep on the couch with *The Little Mermaid* still playing. I smiled and decided not to wake them as I tiptoed out the door.

A thirty-minute ride on the 22 Eastridge line later, I found myself knocking on a screen door. I could see and hear a middle-aged Latino snoring his head off on a nearby sofa and was about to turn back when I heard Jesus call, "Hi Belo," as he opened the screen door and gave me a hug commonly seen only at family reunions. He took my hand and asked me to be quiet as we walked by the sleeping man.

I asked, "Is that your dad?"

He shushed me and said, "No, it's Carlos' and Rodrigo's dad. He is an alkie though."

I walked into a bedroom and saw two thin, well-dressed guys, one on the computer chatting and the other ironing a shirt. Jesus made the introductions, and I could feel all three sets of eyes sizing me up. I wanted to divert their attention from me, and I asked, "So, what are we doing?"

Jesus looked at me like I had three tits and smirked, "*Hell-lo* ... going to a club. You do have an ID, right?"

About a month before, I had found someone else's wallet in the plaza where I worked. I thought it was ironic that the guy and I shared the same birthday, but he was five years older. A firm believer in karma, I mailed his wallet and $32 to the address listed on the license, but kept the ID for myself. I figured I had done a good deed and let that wash my guilt away. I cocked my head and walked to the full-length mirror on the wall to examine my braces and said, "Of course I do."

Jesus walked behind me, placed his hand on my shoulder, and said, "Cool, I knew you would fit right in."

We soon began to crack jokes and sing along to tunes on the radio. I was beginning to feel relaxed when Carlos sneered, "Are you seriously thinking about wearing that shirt?"

I looked down at my red and white-striped shirt and answered, "What's wrong with it?"

Carlos smiled and his braces glimmered under the light. "Um, it's too baggy for you."

I squinted toward Rodrigo and shook my index finger as I said, "He is wearing baggy clothes too."

Jesus and Carlos looked at each other and responded in unison. "He has to, he has no ass."

We all laughed, and Rodrigo flipped us off as he continued to type away in the chat room. Carlos offered to let me wear one of his shirts, and I began to closely scan his face as he buttoned the black short-sleeved Lycra shirt, from some designer I had never heard of, down my chest. Carlos had a strong jaw line and nose, with thick eyebrows and a peaches–and-cream complexion, paler than most of the Mexican guys I knew. His hair was various shades of dark brown that were slicked back, allowing it to fall into natural waves. He could have easily passed for Greek or any type of Mediterranean for that matter.

We all bathed ourselves in different Armani fragrances and jumped into the car. I examined my shirt during the entire hour-long drive south to the 831 area code. I could tell by the cut and fabric, it could have possibly cost what I made in a week. Most importantly, though, Carlos had let me borrow it—something no one had ever done for me. I had no brothers, and none of my straight friends would ever even offer such a thing.

Climbing out of the car, we verified each other's club gear. Jesus fixed my collar, and all three of the guys said, "Belo, you look good." Now my sisters' inspection walks with each other made sense. They were not at all superficial, but moral support.

I stood still as I saw grown men with beards and mustaches make out outside the club. I looked at Jesus and said, "We're going to a gay club?" as I placed my hand on his shoulder like he had done earlier.

Jesus and Carlos both rolled their eyes, and I was surprised to hear Rodrigo say, "Duh, where else can faggots go?" Jesus and Carlos each grabbed on to an arm and said at the same time, "It's okay; we'll teach you."

We got into the club without any problem and slowly made our way to the bar, all three members of my new posse stopping every few seconds to say hello to someone. Jesus whispered into my ear, "You're a hit; wait for this guy on the left to offer you a drink, and ask him to get your friends some too."

As Jesus predicted, an older Latino man wearing a cowboy hat approached me and said, "*Hola, guapo,* can I get you something?"

I looked down at his cowboy boots and said, "My friends and I are having margaritas," and lifted my left brow for a dramatic effect. The guy turned his back to me and walked toward the bar.

Jesus and Carlos patted my back, and Jesus said, "Very good job! You are learning fast, but for the future, we don't drink margaritas, too many carbs. Ask for shots like Grey Goose or Patron."

We danced cumbia and salsa all night, and Carlos and Jesus introduced me to different guys. I was on my third drink when a thin and rather homely go-go dancer stepped on the stage. We all four looked at each other with disappointment, and I said, "Um, he's not worth any of my dollars."

They all nodded and Jesus suggested, "Why don't you jump onstage and show him how it's done."

I almost dropped my Vodka Red Bull when I heard Rodrigo say, "Yeah, Belo, you have a better body."

I had been having so much fun and it was so nice to have found gay boys my age that I jumped on the stage and took off my shirt. A few older men began to stuff bills in the underwear waistband that peeked out from under my jeans.

A tall, heavy man wanted to pull my pants down. I stopped dancing and yelled, "Quit it, dude!" but he continued to pull and had succeeded to get them down to my knees when Jesus, Carlos, and Rodrigo all stepped between the guy and me and pushed him back.

Jesus said, "How about a little respect for our brother?" The guy backed away and faded into the dancing crowed.

I pulled my pants up and realized I had dirtied Carlo's shirt. I said, "Oh my gosh. I messed up your shirt."

Carlos put his arm around me and said, "It's okay, Belo; I didn't buy it anyway. Some guy bought it for me." He pulled me back to our table, telling me about the rules of the gay games. I listened tentatively and eagerly, as I, too, was hoping to become a Gaymer.

6

The Gaymes

Mason looked at me with pain and disappointment. Tears surfaced in his soft brown eyes. I turned away and caught my reflection in the rearview mirror. It was not my first time initiating the end of what I considered a fling, yet I could still see guilt and remorse stamped all over my face. When he stopped in front of my house, I unbuckled my seat belt and jumped out of his Lexus SUV, avoiding eye contact the entire time. I looked at his full lips and said, "Have a safe drive."

I bolted into my house, hoping a warm shower would wash away some of the guilt. Opening the door to my room, I was startled to see a bouquet of white roses sitting on my desk. I rushed to grab the small white card that peeked from the cluster of flowers and quickly became annoyed when I read his name. I then heard my mom's warm tone, "So are those from the basketball player in the Lexus?"

I gave a sarcastic chuckle as I crumpled the piece of paper and mysteriously made the long shot into the garbage bin across the room. I told her that I had decided not to see Mason anymore and that he was not at all a basketball player. I pulled the vase near me and added, "He is so bad at sports; it's not even funny." I could feel a pep talk surfacing, and

I picked a rose from the bouquet and, uninterested in her advice, started to pluck its petals. I said, "These flowers are from this other guy I can't seem to shake off. He's so dumb."

My mom confiscated the flower from my hand and picked up the rest of the bouquet with her other arm. I could see her pale face redden as she scolded me, "Don't play with people's hearts. Be a man! Tell them the truth, and don't lead them on."

My mom would sometimes side with my friends if she thought I was in the wrong, and it irritated the hell out of me. I stared into my fish tank and said, "It's not my fault. They just don't listen when I tell them I'm not interested."

My mom rolled her eyes at me and said, "I won't smack you, because life will smack you harder. I didn't raise you to mistreat anyone."

She stormed out of the room and told me she would burn some lavender incense in my room to help clear my thoughts. I slumped onto my bed and indulged in the calming and forgetful trance of various shades of tropical fish.

The next day Jesus, Carlos, Rodrigo, and I spent most of the afternoon at Valley Fair Mall, shopping for club gear to wear to the legendary Club Papi that evening. Like a celebrity on a concert tour, Club Papi would rotate through various cities from Los Angeles to San Francisco and now to our very own San Jose. I was fixing the collar on a Gucci shirt when I asked my friends. "So, how do you guys shake someone off? I mean, after you have already hung out for a while?"

Jesus was trying on some dark denim pants as he answered, "Duh, change your number. Ignore them in public."

I looked back at Carlos modeling a pair of Prada shades as he chimed in, "You should make out with someone else and be sure they watch. That usually keeps them away." I bit my lower lip trying to picture myself following their advice, but was unable to see myself act like them.

We all used the gift cards we had collected as presents over the past months and made our purchases. Shoving our shopping bags into Rodrigo's trunk, we headed to Carlos' house. I asked the brothers, "Is your mom going to be home?"

Carlos looked back at me from the driver's seat and said, "Nope, she's in Mexico getting a face lift. We have the house to ourselves."

Jesus high-fived Carlos and screamed out the moving car, "It's on, bitches!"

Like cats, we all rose from our pre-club napping spots on the California king bed and began to get ready for Papi. Carlos jumped in the shower, and Jesus started to iron our clothes. I had finished a few sets of push-ups and sit-ups and gave Jesus a hug as he ironed my shirt. "You are the best mom ever!"

He pushed me away and said, "It's Miss Mommy to you, mister." We both laughed, and then I headed to the bathroom to wash up. Jesus was the most domesticated of the group and often ironed and cooked for us. In return, we all helped him out financially when we could. He was kicked out of his house for being gay and was unofficially adopted by the brothers. He was not as attractive as Carlos but somehow possessed the confidence of a supermodel. He could talk strangers into anything and always came up with the most original insults.

We arrived at the San Fernando parking garage and approved each other's outfits before walking the two blocks to the club. San Jose can be as homophobic as cities in the

Midwest, so I was not shocked when I heard a guy yell from his car as we approached Club Papi, "Fuckin' faggots! This ain't Frisco!"

Like many soccer moms do when they hit the brakes suddenly, Jesus extended his arm to protect all three of us and shouted, "Just because your dick gets hard does not make you a man!" Jesus raised his chin up toward the stars in the sky, and we all followed him inside.

I felt like I was at the premiere of a big Hollywood movie. I met guys from as far as New York and Miami who had flown in for the Papi event. There were porn stars, multiple dance floors, and cute waiters serving drinks I had never heard of before. I was in line to have my picture taken with one of the adult models when I felt someone pull my arm and ask, "Did you get the roses I sent?" I sensed my throat tightening and looked back at his green eyes. I scanned the room for the guys as he pulled me into his chest and asked, "Why don't you talk to me? First, you are telling me I'm the best kisser, and then you disappear on me." I thought back to what Carlos had said earlier and reached out into the crowd of dancing bodies and pulled a guy toward me and kissed him on the lips. I looked back and saw Green Eyes' face hurt as he disappeared into the flashing lights and smoke.

I realized I was still holding on to my lifesaver and turned back to face him. He was an older man with a few strands of silver hair slicked back. He adjusted his black frames, and I could now notice the crow's feet that were magnified from behind the lenses. He smiled and said, "Hi there. You are amazing; that kiss was like, bonkers." I smiled and retreated to the smoking area.

I stopped Jesus getting a light from a guy wearing a beret and ran toward him. "This guy got all crazy with me. We should go home."

The guy in the beret took a step back, and Jesus blew smoke rings into the air. Hat guy said, "Wow, that's some major mouth power."

Annoyed with the stranger, I pulled Jesus to the side. I saw Carlos nearby and signaled him toward us. I began to explain to both of them that this guy who liked me would not leave me alone. Carlos said, "That old guy you kissed? I thought you were just drunk."

Before I could say anything, I saw Green Eyes peer from behind Jesus and Carlos. He pushed them aside, and he said, "Just tell me it's over, and I will leave you alone."

Jesus and Carlos both stepped in front of the guy, and Jesus said, "He doesn't want to talk to you. Get a clue!"

He said, "Fuck you, Belo!" and stormed away. I was haunted by the pain in his green eyes, and I felt my own begin to water.

Jesus slapped me and said, "Don't fuckin' cry. Here, shake it off, and kill my drink."

Carlos had made friends with the club owner and, in minutes, brought him to me. "I'm sorry you're not having fun. Don't worry. I'll have the guy kicked out right away." Carlos and the club owner disappeared, and in a few moments, I saw the security guys escorting Green Eyes away.

I told Jesus and Carlos how bad I felt for not being up-front with the guy. I knew I was wrong to lead him on, and my mom's words came back to me. They both nodded their heads, and Carlos said, "You're not wrong." It suddenly hit me: whether I was wrong or not, the guys would always have my back.

7

Gayme Over

The drumming, clapping, and singing began to speed up, and I yawned twice before shaking Claribel's hand. I was too tired to attempt any acrobatics and limited my movements to basic kicks. Unfortunately, Claribel was full of energy, and after a few sequences of kicks and flips, I started to cough as I struggled to keep up with her. I saw the petite Filipina girl jump in the air, and too tired to register the kick, I was startled by her foot slapping my chin. The crowd of men and women who circled us gasped, and I began to feel my skin burn. Mestre Vaginho had the same shocked look I must have had. And by the curl in his lower lip, I could tell we were both thinking the same thing. How could someone training for as many years as I and holding a yellow belt not duck or flee from such a commonly used kick? I shook Claribel's hand and ran to the bathroom. I splashed my face with cold water and dabbed my broken lip with tissue paper. I heard the Portuguese lyrics come to a sudden stop as Mestre Vaginho yelled to announce the Capoeira game was over.

I timidly opened the bathroom door and saw the white uniformed bodies seated Indian style on the wooden floor. I tiptoed into the circle and found a spot next to Claribel. Mestre Vaginho was announcing the Batizado belting ceremony as he unstrung a Berimbau. Claribel leaned into my ear as she tied her long black hair into a ponytail. "Sorry, Belo, are you okay?"

Although my lip still burned, I lied and said, "I'm cool. Don't trip." Everyone around me listened tentatively while Vaginho informed us his master would be flying from Brazil for the event. He waved a piece of paper in the air with the names of the people who would receive belts. He taped the sheet of paper to the wall and like actors after an audition, all the students crowded around the list to see if they had made it. Claribel skipped in my direction and excitedly told me she would be getting her yellow/green belt.

Many Capoeira schools follow the belting system established by the Capoeira Federation in Brazil, which only has four student belts: green, yellow/green, yellow, and yellow/blue. The fifth belt, which is blue, means the Capoeirista has graduated and can begin teaching. The crowd had dwindled down, and I stepped toward the list and eagerly began to scan the names. I noticed the yellow/blue category had only two names. Seeing my name missing made me want to throw up. I stared at the list in shock as everyone headed to the dressing rooms to change. Out of the corner of my eye, I could see Mestre Vaginho coming toward me, and in a few seconds, he placed his arm around me.

"You are a good Capoeirista, but the last year, you've become distant. It's almost as if you're checked out," he said in his heavily accented English. I remained quiet, knowing perfectly well he was right. The last year of clubbing and drinking had displaced my goal of getting my blue belt. He embraced me tightly and smacked the back of my head as he said, "Maybe next time! Go change."

I stepped out of the dressing room and smiled when I saw Rodrigo seated in the spectator area. I walked up to him and gave him a big hug. "Wow, you came. Thanks!" We left the Capoeira school and began to drive to Rodrigo's house. I asked, "So, what do you think about Capoeira?"

He looked back at me, keeping both hands on the steering wheel, and responded, "It's okay. You are pretty good. Didn't know you could do back handsprings." I accepted his compliment and smiled, knowing he did not see my best game. Rodrigo sighed and told me he would not be going out with us that night.

"What? But it's Friday!" He rubbed his eyes and said he was too tired to go out. I could tell there was something bothering him.

"Okay, so what is really going on with you?" We pulled into his driveway, and he paused for a few seconds, withdrawing the key from the ignition.

"I'm tired of being single. You all get so much attention, but no one really talks to me. I'm just over going out for a while." Not knowing what to say, I remained quiet, and we headed inside the house.

From the sofa, Jesus asked, "Hey, you. How was your class?" I gave Carlos and Jesus a hug and told them about not getting my yellow/blue belt.

Carlos grabbed me a second time and said, "Oh, you'll be fine. Nothing a little dancin' can't cure."

Jesus rose from the couch and said, "It will be just you three tonight," dashing into his room. Carlos and I both looked at each other and followed him into the room. Jesus pulled an Armani shirt out of the closet and showed it to both of us as Rodrigo peeked in the room and said, "I'm going to bed. Not feelin' it tonight."

We heard Rodrigo's door slam, and I filled the guys in on what was going on with him. Carlos said, "It's okay; I'll drive my car tonight then."

Jesus modeled his new shirt in front of the mirror and said, "I have a boyfriend, and I'm going to the movies with him tonight." Carlos and I both stared back at Jesus, puzzled. Jesus had told us that Cisco was not his type but that he was really nice and had bought him a cell phone.

Carlos and I insisted he come with us, but Jesus would not budge, "Sorry, bitches, but I'm off the market and the club scene."

Dragging our feet to Carlos' room, we lounged around not saying a word. Carlos jumped off the bed, and in a few seconds, I began to hear the chimes from instant messages. I said, "What are you up to?" Carlos remained quiet, and I leaned over his shoulder and saw a picture of a very attractive Latin guy, "Day-um, who is that?"

Carlos looked back at me with a coy smile, "That is my date for tonight. He says his friend thinks you're cute. It will be a double date." We had plenty of group pictures by now, and I figured Carlos had emailed the guy pictures from the previous Pride weekend. I was still wearing my Capoeira uniform and began to look through Carlos' closet. Carlos said, "You should wear my short-sleeved Kenneth Cole shirt; you know, the black one. It will look good on you."

I smiled back at him as I buttoned the shirt. "So, where are we meeting these guys at?"

Carlos was changing into a white Guess shirt as he answered, "Norma Jean's."

Carlos had not been an active driver for very long, and I grew worried as I saw the winding road in my mind.

"Are you sure you want to drive that far? Why can't we go to TD's or Mac's?"

Carlos rolled his eyes before answering, "Those places are lame, and you know Norma Jean's plays better music."

I felt uneasy about driving in bad weather down such narrow and dark roads. However, I didn't say anything, since I knew Carlos was trying to salvage the night.

We walked out of the house and were saluted by a misty gust of wind. My eyes began to water, and I rushed to get into his fire-red Civic. Carlos set the radio to a Spanish station, and in a few minutes, we were speeding down the freeway. After driving for a half hour, the road became pitch dark, and the only light was coming from the car's high beams. I asked Carlos, "Can you slow down? It's so narrow here."

Carlos responded, "We're fine. I want to get to the club before they start the drag show."

I figured I should just let him focus on the road, and I started to hum along with a tune on the radio. Highway 17 was tough to navigate in daylight; for an inexperienced driver to attempt the drive at night was pretty bold. The radio signal faded, and I began to search for another station. I had my eyes on the dial when I heard Carlos scream, "Oh shit!"

I looked up and saw bushes and branches coming at us. The seat belt tightened, and my head was yanked back into the headrest. I closed my eyes, and when I opened them, everything was dark. Carlos put his hand on my shoulder and asked, "Are you okay?"

We both opened our doors slowly, and I walked toward the front of the car. "How could you hit the side of a hill?" I shouted.

Carlos looked up at me from his examination of the car and said, "This is your fault. If you weren't singing so loud, I wouldn't have gotten distracted."

I was startled by the anger in his voice and refrained from snapping back when one of Mestre Vaginho's sayings surfaced in my mind. He once told me after a Capoeira game,

"When you let someone upset you, they take your power away."

Turning my back to him, I pulled out my cell phone and attempted to call someone to come get me. My phone had no reception. "Damn it!" I yelled at the shadowy trees that danced along with the wind.

Carlos put his arms around me, "I'm sorry. I am just freaked out." We both sighed and went back to inspect the car. There were very minimal scratches on the hood, and it appeared to be running fine.

I chuckled, "This is crazy! There are only two scratches on the driver's side after such a big bang." Carlos smiled, and although I was still shaking, I jumped back into the car to finish the drive.

"We're only five minutes away," Carlos said. "We're just gonna hang out for a bit, then go back home." I nodded and resisted turning the radio on and humming to keep myself calm.

We arrived at the bar and were greeted by a group of thirtysomethings. They whistled at us, and Carlos whispered into my ear, "See, we are fine, just the two of us. We're the better-looking ones anyway."

I rolled my eyes at a heavyset man missing a tooth who blew me a kiss from inside the club. Carlos grabbed my hand and stuck his tongue out at the toothless guy. We found our dates, and after a few introductions, Carlos and his guy disappeared onto the dim dance floor.

My date had a shaved head and a goatee and was already pretty drunk. Not moving up in Capoeira, getting into a car crash, and getting stuck with a drunk all seemed like a very bad dream. My chest felt sore, and I excused myself to go to the bathroom. The fluorescent light over the sink began to flicker as I washed my hands and unbuttoned my shirt. I felt a shiver down my nape when I saw the red and purple belt print on my chest. It was not until I saw my damaged skin that I realized how close I had been to gayme over.

8

Edges

It had been three eternal and painful months of learning to see again. The first surgery in my right eye had more fruitful results than any doctor had hoped or anticipated. I went from seeing shadows dancing in a foggy pool to being able to see color again and eventually to being able to read print. Although the vision I gained was not strong enough to permit me to drive, I did not qualify for any blind-related services and hid all the adaptive equipment given to me in a bag under my bed. It was like a sky full of fireworks and hundreds of champagne bottles popping the day I stopped using my hands to move and began to trust my sight again. I used to sit by the bay window that hovers over Mission Street for hours, drunk with joy as every day the vibrant picture became more detailed. I would gently massage my eye, thanking it for defying blindness as I softly smiled at the numerous bodies adorning the buzzing block.

One icy San Francisco morning, I was awoken from my slumber by the city's breath on the side of my face. Drowsily, I fought the blankets off my body and snailed my way through the room. The molding that wraps itself around the window welcomed me back. I was stunned that I had not seen it and began to fiercely blink. It seemed like someone had rubbed

Vaseline all over the double-paned glass. I poked my head into a gust of wind and was petrified when all I could see were shades of gray. I turned my face toward where I believed my dresser guarded my phone. I charged forward only to find the wall and landed on my back after its force pushed me down to the carpet. I sat up and attempted to scrape up the remains of any vision by trying to focus. I caught a glimpse of a chocolate-brown piece of furniture and army-crawled toward my cell phone's captor. I stretched my hand as far as I possibly could without losing my arm and found the coveted item amid the clutter. Shakily, I dialed my doctor.

The California Pacific Medical Center had become like a second home over recent months. Similar to a six-year-old kid who memorizes his home number, the digits came back to me in the form of a rhyme. A woman answered the phone, and before she could finish her greeting, I yelled, "I can't see. I can't see. I can't see!" I struggled to answer her basic and routine questions, as I nervously glided my fingers across my now-soaked face.

A few moments later, Dr. Wong came to the phone and cleared his throat before asking, "What's wrong, Mr. Cipriani?"

I responded dejectedly, "It's gone; it's all cloudy again."

I could hear him breathing as he said, "Your retina may have detached over night. It happens to patients with severe eye trauma like yourself. However, I cannot be certain until I see you here at the clinic."

I nodded and then agreed to take the next cab to the hospital and pressed the END key on my cell.

I held the tiny phone so tightly, I was afraid I was going to break it. I called for a taxi and was told it would be an hour wait, since it was peak traffic time. I tilted my head toward my right shoulder and realized that I caught a watery glimpse of my closet door. Like a passenger aboard a plane about to crash, I began to panic. I slowly gathered myself from the floor and, with my hands stretched out in front of me, began to move around my room. I reached my closet and was consumed by fright as I struggled to see the colors of the different garments. I ripped the hanger off what looked to be a red-hooded sweater and wrestled it on. I also found some dark-colored denim pants and struggled into those too. I stumbled my way to the living room where I found a pair of flip-flops and slipped them on. I shifted my head from side to side, trying as hard as I could to catch bits of the terra-cotta painted walls and yellow wooden floors. I ran my hand on the bottom of the TV and managed to turn it on. I saw fuzzy images on the screen move around and stroked the glass with my index finger as I said goodbye.

The cab driver rang my bell as if he was announcing a winner, yet it became clear the battle had been lost. I slithered toward the door and caught sight of the mirror hanging near it. I was stunned to see my blurry reflection and paused as I watched my image fade into the mirror's surface.

9

Shades of Gray

"This doesn't taste like chamomile!" I shouted.

"It also has lemongrass," answered my mom in a soft voice from the kitchen.

"Just because I can't see doesn't mean I can't figure things out. I'm not dumb!" I answered in an adolescent tone. The acidic words burned my tongue slightly as they passed my lips and bounced in the room. I heard my mom's rubber shoes shuffle on the wooden floor, then felt her hand push my curls away from my face. I swooshed the tea in my mouth a few times and, in a calmer voice, said, "It also has mint." I wiped a heavy tear with my left hand and gave out a sarcastic chuckle. I heard my cell vibrate on the placemat, and I swallowed the herbal water before answering. My mother patted my head, attempting to knock some of the anger out of my voice, and went back to the kitchen.

"Hi, Belo, it's Jason from the Law Offices of Elizabeth Berger. How did your doctor's appointment go?" he asked.

"Bad. Really bad. My retina detached again," I replied.

"I'm really sorry to hear that, Belo. What else did the doctor say?"

I answered, "They're going to try a third time. The surgery

I had two weeks ago failed, and I stopped seeing lights. My next surgery is already scheduled for next week. It will be covered by the Lions Eye Foundation. It was all handled this morning."

His voice slowed as he added apologetically, "I don't have great news either."

His tone sent a jolt through me, "What happened?"

"Well, SFPD has dropped the criminal case."

"What! Why?" I demanded.

"We were not able to get any witnesses, video, or pictures that place the Lopez brothers at the crime scene. However, you still have a strong shot at a civil case."

I felt my esophagus shrink and slowly bit my lower lip before answering. The images of my assault came rushing back into my head, like trailers from a movie I never auditioned for. I felt my anger penetrating my skin. "That's ridiculous. Is that the reason why they've not been found?" I demanded.

"We hired a servicing company. They seem not to live or work in the places we have for them."

I took a deep breath before uttering a shaky "okay."

He continued in a professional tone, "I'll continue with the civil case and keep you posted, Belo."

Giving out a hopeless "thank you," I hit the power button on my phone.

I fled from the dining table to the wall and trailed it toward my room, shouting to my mom, "I'm not hungry anymore. I need to go rest."

My mom didn't try to follow me, and I arrived in my room and closed the door behind me. I jumped into bed and began to curse Carlos. I could not believe that the assholes who had inflicted so much pain, and who were clearly guilty, were still free. I furiously blinked and waved my hand in front of me. It felt inhuman to feel my eyelids blink and my eyeballs move but not be able to see. I thought that my legal case, like my vision, had unjustly gone all gray.

10

Unicorns

I woke up with the worst hangover in the world; however, it was not liquor that I consumed the previous day, but high levels of anesthesia. This was the medical team's fourth attempt at reattaching my retina and, based on Dr. Hopkins's tone of voice, my last opportunity at gaining back any sight. I was in a haze as my mom and sister prepared me to return to the hospital for a postsurgery follow-up. The ride to the California Pacific Medical Center felt brief, as I fell into a drowsy sleep as soon as my head touched the car seat. The operations had become routine, and like a high-functioning drunk, I learned to relax and move in my trance. The nurses—who, over the past seven months, had become more than acquaintances—greeted me as soon as I set foot in the lobby. Before my sister could find us chairs, we were moved to an exam room.

Dr. Hopkins came into the room shortly after I had gotten comfortable in the examination chair. I heard running water and the crumpling of paper towels as he said, "Hi, Mr. Cipriani. Let's check things out." His cold fingers began to gently remove my bandages, and I felt liquid roll down my face. He dabbed the sticky tears and asked, "Can you see my fingers?"

I struggled to swallow for a few seconds before answering, "No, it's all black. It's darker than last time."

I heard him move some tools around and ask, "Can you see the light?"

I let out a faint "no."

I then felt his breath on my face as he said, "The main goal of this procedure was to save your eye and maintain a healthy anatomy. Your retina is attached, and you may be a candidate for future procedures. As for now, I suggest you contact the LightHouse for the Blind. I'm really sorry, Belo."

I felt a sharp pain in my throat that burned as it made its way down my chest and into my stomach. Dr. Hopkins excused himself. He tapped my shoulder, and I heard him close the door behind him. My mom and sister both hugged me. I became aware of the rage making its way through every vein in my body and stuttered my attackers' names, beginning to produce the most toxic tears in my life.

I spent the next week in bed, trying to sleep as much as possible. I told my friends and family, "I need to sleep, because in my dreams, I can still see." Everyone allowed me to fall into an abyss of depression and bitterness. I spent the next month avoiding phone calls, since so many people repeating "I'm sorry" felt hollow and scripted.

One day, about a month after my doomsday prognosis, my mom came into my room and asked, "When are you getting up? It's 1:00 PM."

"I feel so ugly. I am a blind faggot; I might as well be a unicorn." I added, "Can you see this?" and pointed at my forehead, not expecting a response.

"That's not a horn; it's a pimple," she said.

"Well, it feels like a damn horn."

She responded gently, "Unicorns are very pretty and special, Belo. You're not the first blind man. You should call that blind school." Her intervention went between Spanish and Portuguese, sprinkling in a little English, but I saw the light in all three tongues. I gave in and dialed the LightHouse for the Blind on Van Ness Avenue.

I started to think about all the blind people I saw traveling alone on Muni and the city's crooked streets and began to accept the fact that I could also learn to use those white sticks and read the bumps on the ATMs. I remembered talking to a guy named Bryce immediately following the attack, but I had never returned his calls, since my vision improved temporarily during that time. The woman who answered at the Light-House switchboard transferred me to him. He picked up the line after the first ring and told me about the programs they offered. He remembered talking to me a few months earlier, but he never asked about my reasons for not calling back. Ten minutes into the conversation, I said, "Bryce, you should also know I'm gay, and that it makes my situation even more unique. I know. I'm a unicorn."

Bryce laughed, responding, "Well, I'm a unicorn too." He answered my surprise with, "Oh yeah, I'm blind and gay, but I have a partner who's sighted and doesn't mind my condition. There are many blind gay men in the area. You might even meet some here at the LightHouse."

I hung up the phone and walked toward my bay window. For the first time in over a month, I felt the solar energy bestowing me with new hope.

11

Cookin' without Lookin'

"How will I be able to pick my clothes?" I asked.

"Well, they have Braille labels you can sew on your clothes," responded Laurie, my new social worker at the LightHouse. "They also have these small devices called color identifiers that you hold over the surface of your clothing, which tell you what color they are."

"Ooh, that's really cool," I said.

"Dan Spinelli, the cooking teacher, and I will be stopping by this afternoon to label your house, sign paperwork, and answer any questions that you may have," said Laurie.

"Okay, see you later," I said and hung up the line.

I walked to my closet and ran my fingers across the fabrics as if I were playing the piano. My family had separated my clothes, hanging light colors on the left and dark colors on the right; however, I still felt unsure about coordinating outfits together. Although I was entirely aware that both Laurie and Dan were blind, I wanted to dress up for them. I was tired of wearing sweats and strongly believed that my first encounter with other blind people should not go without any proper preparation. I felt for a pair of jeans, and then I reached for a dress shirt from the darker palate side and began to get ready.

I dug through the cabinet drawer that I remembered stored my hairstyling products. I opened up a few bottles and carefully sniffed. Although I had only been blind a few months, I had already learned the careful sniffing technique to avoid any tragic surprises. Each plastic container I smelled reminded me of different aspects of my sighted self, a part of me that now felt like a past life: the citrus scent of the heavy-hold gel that took me back to late nights in SOMA and the vanilla light-hold mousse that had accompanied me every morning on BART for my commute to work.

I was running warm water on my hands, trying to remove the hair product from my skin when I heard my cell ring. My damp finger hit the answer button, and I said, "Hello, Laurie?"

"Hi, Belo; it's Dan. We can't find the entrance to your building. Can you come get us?"

"Oh, um, I'm not sure I can," I replied. Then, I became annoyed with myself. I could not believe I wasn't able to help people find my apartment. I said, "I can ring my intercom, which will buzz you in and make a loud sound."

"Okay, that works," Dan answered.

I pressed down on the rectangular button on the side of the speaker box as if I knew the answer to a question on Jeopardy. I heard footsteps on the stairwell and stepped out barefoot into the hallway outside my condo. I asked, "Dan, is that you? Um, Laurie?"

His voice came back to me, "Belo? Keep talking; we're coming," I heard plastic bags and feet dragging at the end of the hall.

I said, "Thanks for coming. I know my place is in a noisy area. Not very blind friendly, I guess."

Laurie replied, "Nonsense, you're in a great location. Buses, stores, it's actually going to make things easier for mobility." She finished her sentence and placed her soft hand in mine, "Nice to meet you, Belo."

A bigger and rugged hand moved in right after she withdrew hers. "Hi, Belo, Dan here. Nice to meet you."

We walked inside my apartment, and I said, "My table is to the left." I tapped the tabletop twice and pulled out a chair.

Dan said, "What a beautiful piece of furniture! Is this a mini bar?"

"Oh yeah, it's an antique," I added. I thought it was amazing he was able to locate the wooden piece so quickly.

Laurie added, "What beautiful colors you have on your walls, Belo."

I was puzzled by their comments and asked, "Laurie, I thought you guys were blind?"

"We are; my vision is 2200, which makes me legally blind," Dan answered.

"I have a little bit of vision too," Laurie said.

"How much can you see, Laurie?" I asked.

"I can see shapes and colors but with very little detail," Laurie answered. I was stunned and began to feel like the fattest kid at fat camp.

"Can you see movement? Do you have any light perception?" Dan asked.

"Not anymore. I lost it all after my last surgery. I'm a total," I replied.

"The karma those guys have coming to them. They have no idea," Dan said.

"Belo, let's get started," Laurie interjected.

I heard Dan walk into my kitchen, and Laurie began to collect a few signatures from me. "I have this plastic item here called a signature guide. Just sign inside the box," she said. Laurie also pulled out a square object the size of an answering machine and explained, "This is a Braille display."

I gently pressed my fingers on a smooth surface and felt bumps raised from the plastic. "Is this Braille?" I asked.

"Yes, it is," she responded. "There are many cool blind toys now."

From the kitchen, I heard Dan call out, saying, "Okay, Belo, I want to show you a few things." I got up and slowly walked to my kitchen. "Let's start with the microwave," Dan added when he heard me enter the kitchen.

"I can't use the microwave, because it has a completely flat panel, no buttons for me to feel," I said.

"Not for long," he responded, "I'm adding bump dots."

"Is that Braille?" I asked.

"Nope, they are just adhesive bumps. They're clear and easily removed." He grabbed my hand, and I smiled when my fingers found the bump he indicated; it felt like the eraser end of a pencil. "This bump is now power," he added. He began to label and explain each button as he went along.

"What are you going to have him make, Dan?" Laurie asked as she walked in the kitchen.

"A potato, then a hot dog," he replied.

Dan placed a fork in my hand and pushed it over the potato. He had me punch a few holes into it with a fork. I gingerly placed the potato in a ceramic bowl, then in the microwave. "You're doing really well, Belo," Dan said.

"Did you cook when you were sighted?" Laurie asked.

"Very little. I'm a great bartender though," I answered.

"That can come in very handy," she replied. We all chuckled as I hit a quick combination of keys on my new microwave. I proceeded to fill a pot with water and turn my stove on. Dan handed me a wooden spoon and said, "Belo, treat this spoon as if it were your cane."

"He hasn't had any mobility yet, Dan," Laurie chimed in.

Dan grabbed my hand and had me feel around the pot

sitting over the flame. "Use this technique to make sure the pot is on right and won't tip over," he said.

"You should be getting a call from one of the mobility instructors soon, Belo," Laurie added.

"Ummm," I murmured, trying really hard to concentrate on putting the hot dog in the pot.

Dan placed a fork in my hand and a plate on the counter. "Belo, you're going to take them out once you hear the water boiling," he said. I felt like a teenager being dared by his friends to jump off a roof. One of the biggest fears I had as a blind man was getting hurt. I knew that following Dan's directions was taking the first step in a long journey. I heard the water gargling, and I quickly used the wooden spoon to trail the top of the pot and cautiously stabbed inside the hot metal. I was successful in pulling all three wieners out without burning myself. I wiped the sweat off my forehead. Both Laurie and Dan tapped my shoulder as I resumed a normal breathing pattern. Dan said, "Let's eat! I can do the rest, Belo."

I took a step away from the stove and made my way back to the dining room table. Laurie joined me and Dan followed with the food. "Do you cook, Laurie?" I asked.

"Absolutely! I love it, especially after I find some good stuff at the farmer's market," she answered.

"Great job, Belo!" Dan shouted as he fixed our hot dogs.

"Maybe I can have a cooking show now," I said, with a cheesy smile.

"What would you call it?" asked Laurie.

"Umm, *Cookin' without Lookin'*?" I answered as I happily enjoyed my simple meal in the dark.

12

Citizen Cane

I slowly shifted my feet toward my CD player and hit a square button until I came across a local hip-hop station. I raised the volume and began to cry as I struggled to button my pants. I resumed a normal breathing pattern after I began to feel light-headed and thought I would pass out. I took the jeans off and put them in a plastic bag that harbored the rest of the clothing that refused to fit. I rubbed my face with my T-shirt and felt ashamed of my body. The last nine months of surgeries had kept me in bed for weeks and morphed my body into something that felt unfamiliar to my fingertips. My cell phone began to ring, and I quickly answered with a brisk "Hello."

A kind voice responded, "Hi, Belo. My name is Kristine Thomson, and I'm a mobility instructor at the LightHouse." I then smiled as I remembered the conversations with Dan and Laurie during my intake the previous day.

I banged my knee on a drawer that I forgot I left open and let out an aggravated "Damn it!"

"Are you okay?" Kristine asked politely.

"Um, I, um, hold on please." I trailed my index finger on the side of my CD player and hit the round power button as

I rubbed my knee with the hand holding the phone. I cleared my throat before saying, "Okay, I'm back. I had to turn off the music."

Kristine said, "No problem. I wanted to set up a time for us to get together and work on some mobility."

I replied quickly, "Okay."

"Does today or tomorrow work for you?" Kristine asked.

I nodded as I said, "Yup, I can do today."

"Oh, and one more thing, what is your height and weight?" I felt my stomach knot as I rubbed my hand over my belly. I felt like the black and white before shot on the Jenny Craig commercials. Before I could say anything, she added, "I need to match you to the right-sized cane."

I quickly replied, "I'm five feet eight and weighed one hundred and sixty-five pounds prior to my last surgery, which was a few months ago. Honestly, I probably have gained twenty to twenty-five pounds since then though."

"Do you walk around your neighborhood very much?" Kristine questioned.

"No, not really," I responded. "I get dizzy and don't feel safe outside my apartment."

"Are you free this afternoon?" Kristine asked.

"Yup, I'm totally free. Actually, now that I don't have to see the doctor as much, I have a lot more time on my hands."

"I understand. I will come by your place this afternoon around 2:00 PM," Kristine said in a very patient tone. I hung up the phone and threw on a pair of loose-fitting windbreaker pants that made a shuffling sound as I made my way to the kitchen.

I was living alone as my mom and sister still had their place in San Jose. Most of my meals were prepared by my family and stored in the fridge. However, I would sometimes run out and then would eat pieces of bread with cheese and fruit. I had also memorized my credit card number and resorted to delivery frequently. Cold pizza and a glass of juice had become a staple for me.

I grabbed a box of Cheerios, a soda, and a few pieces of string cheese, and I made myself comfortable on the sofa bed that, for no particular reason, had the mattress extended. On the TV remote, I quickly found the power button, since it was conveniently shaped differently than the rest of the buttons and located on the top right corner. I knew the button was red but now relied on the grooves around the key to find it. I began to listen to the news as I enjoyed my attempt at a breakfast, occasionally taking breaks from chewing, since I was not able to hear the newscaster's voice while I had food in my mouth.

I took a sip of my drink and almost spit out the diet cola taste that took over my tongue. I then remembered my mother had left the diet sodas she drinks because she is diabetic and realized I had accidentally picked up one of her cans. I took a deep breath as I sighed, thinking there was no way I could tell my Sprite from her Diet Coke unless I opened and tasted each of them, which could turn into a big project. I drank the rest of the soda as if I were taking vodka shots and began to relax and disengage myself from the conversations coming from the screen.

I was startled by my doorbell, realizing I had fallen asleep. I jumped up and heard a voice saying, "It's Kristine!" coming out of the intercom.

I buzzed her in and put a sweater on as I heard a set of footsteps make their way up the stairs and then down the hallway that led to my apartment. Knocking followed, and I took a deep breath before opening the door and saying, "Hi, Kristine; come in."

She responded with a warm, "Hi, Belo; it's so good to meet you. What a beautiful place." I smiled as I gently removed a strand of hair from my face and carefully tucked it behind my ear.

I cautiously asked, "Are we gonna take the bus today?"

"No, not today. We'll just work around your building this time." I felt movement coming from where Kristine was standing and then heard a zipper and something snapping. "I have your cane, Belo. I thought we would try a folding one first," said Kristine.

I reached my hand out and wrapped my fingers around the rubber grip. I felt my heart racing as I slid the cane side to side in front of me. I was fully aware that I was holding the visual evidence that made my blindness official. I sighed as I embraced my new fate in the shape of a stick, pushing away all the fears that had been previously holding me back.

Kristine regained my attention by saying, "You look good; let's practice walking down your hallway."

I used my cane to walk out into the corridor and was surprised to realize how much faster I could move. It felt bizarre to touch things with my cane and automatically create a visual. I glided the tip of the cane on the floor and immediately saw the wooden boards in my mind. I felt the threshold and knew I would be making a right to exit my condo. Kristine had me walk from one end of the hallway to the other, giving me pointers along the way. For the first time in months, I felt connected with my surroundings and no longer invisible. I laughed as I said, "I feel like Mr. Peanut."

"Maybe we should get you a top hat," Kristine answered. She ended our lesson by saying, "You did very well, Belo. When are you scheduled to go to the LightHouse?"

I vented to her for a few minutes about how overwhelmed I was with all the social workers and programs I applied to.

"It can get pretty confusing, but you're doing a great job in managing all of the chaos," she replied sympathetically.

We scheduled a second lesson for the following week, and I slowly closed the door behind her. I folded my cane, telling my new stick, "I will call you Citizen Cane."

13

A LightHouse

I sat on my couch tapping my right foot on the wooden floor, eagerly waiting for the cab driver to ring my doorbell. It felt no different from any other first day of school I could remember. Just like in high school, I had coordinated my clothes the previous night to avoid any wardrobe mishaps. I was also sporting a new haircut my friend Sara had taught me to style over the weekend. The cab driver only had to ring the buzzer once, and I jumped up and quickly made my way downstairs. I was still amazed by how much faster I could move with my cane and smiled as the tip glided over each surface I walked on. I felt the grooves on the tile and reached out for the door. A raspy male voice greeted me briskly and escorted me into the cab.

I fastened my seat belt and allowed myself to enjoy the warm air coming out of the vents. I heard the driver snap his seat belt, and the car began to move. The driver asked, "So, we're going to the LightHouse?"

"Yes!" I replied with glee, almost suggesting he hurry. He then began to ask the same set of tired questions asked by social workers, counselors, and random strangers in the hospital waiting area. I responded even before he could wrap up his two-part question with, "I was assaulted last April, and they have not caught the guys." I am not sure if it was my tone or if he was simply disinterested with my story, but he remained silent. I laid my head on the vinyl headrest and disengaged myself from the noises all around me. I shifted my focus to my first day at the LightHouse and imagined what my classes would be like. I pictured a college setting with auditorium-style seating and all the cool talking toys to make learning feasible. Based on the glimpse Laurie and Dan had given me into the blind world, it seemed that there was some nifty way of doing everything without vision. I no longer feared blindness, as I now knew capable and intelligent blind individuals.

My moment of reflection was disturbed by the driver saying, "It's eighteen dollars."

I pulled a bill out of my pants pocket and asked, "Is this a twenty?" He snagged the paper money out of my hand and replaced it with two crisp bills. I grew annoyed as I noted he ignored my question, I assumed I was holding two one dollar bills; however, I still expected an answer. Before I could form a sentence, I heard the door open and felt a cold gust of wind push the side of my face. The driver reached over and unbuckled me. I felt a set of long fingers cup my arm, as I was yanked out of the warm car and into the misty street. I asked a second time, "How much is this?" and waved the bills in front of me.

"It's two dollars," he replied as he dragged me down the block. The man continued to jerk me down the street, and I began to feel like a child being dragged home by a parent. My annoyance moved into anger as he placed my hand over a glass door and said, "You're here."

I felt rage coat my face, and I crumpled the bills into my coat pocket. I turned around and yelled toward the traffic, "Fuck you, Carlos!" I was stunned to hear his name burst out of my mouth and took a deep breath to calm myself. I contemplated going back home until I realized I did not know the way back or have the ability to hail a cab on my own.

I heard a guy say, "Are you looking for the button?" I turned toward the voice and nodded. I had no idea what button he referred to; I was just grateful to be acknowledged. The door made a popping sound and opened slightly. I pushed the door and stepped inside the building. I heard the man walk in behind me and say, "I'm here to pick up Ms. Stewart."

A young woman confidently cried, "That's me. Mina, let's go." I heard heels tap the marble floor and then felt something wet against my hand. I realized that Mina was a guide dog and quickly reached into my pocket, beyond the wrinkled bills, and found my hand sanitizer. I figured there was no better way to start my day than to be tethered to a cold stranger and end up with drool on my hand.

A woman nearby asked, "And who are you here to see?"

I hesitated to answer, since I was not sure if she was talking to me. "Um, I'm here for class; my name is Belo."

"Oh, hi, Belo! I'm Diana; you're in my Vision Loss class," she said as she walked toward me. "Here, take my arm."

I noticed Diana walked at the same relaxed, confident, and carefree pace my sighted family did and was overtaken by curiosity. I asked without any hesitation, "Are you blind?"

"I have a bit of sight," she answered politely. Diana seated me on a soft-cushioned chair and said, "We're going to start in five minutes; just hang out for a bit." I didn't say anything, since I was still getting over the fact that I had met yet another blind person who could see. I thought back to those months where I had a bit of sight and realized I had been blind all along. I became restless as I wondered where I would be if I had accepted my blindness then.

The room began to fill up with voices, yet I remained lost in my self-pity. I heard Dan's voice say, "Hi, Belo!" and I pushed my emotions aside. I smiled as I figured he could see my teeth.

Diana quieted the room by introducing herself and telling us about her eye condition. "I have something called Retinitis Pigmentosa," she announced for all to hear. I was amazed with how comfortable she felt with sharing that information with a group of people. It was as if someone had asked for her major in college or her astrological sign. Dan then asked for everyone to introduce themselves and share the cause of their blindness.

After the ice breaker ran its course, I realized I was the only totally blind individual in the class. During the break, I became bothered as all the other students tried to help me walk to the kitchen for a snack. They all zipped around me, offering coffee, fruit, or milk. I did not know how old anyone was, but based on their voices, they all seemed like baby boomers. We headed back to class and discussed labeling and telephones. Dan said, "Do you guys know all phones including cells have a raised bump on the number five?"

I reached in my coat pocket and felt for my phone. I stroked the buttons and counted them until I got to five. I chuckled when I found the little raised dot in the middle of the keypad. A woman to my left asked, "What's so funny, Belo?"

I said, "This whole time I've been counting the buttons, driving myself crazy trying not to miscount a key."

Another female voice echoed, "Me too!"

We all laughed and Dan chimed with, "That's why we're all here, to learn from one another. I even sometimes have students show me new tricks."

It was in this moment that I realized that it did not matter how much sight someone else in my class displayed—we were all there to learn the same skills and struggled in the same manner. I also accepted the idea that although Carlos and the other jerks had landed me in the LightHouse, it was where I belonged for the time being. I asked Dan, "Can blind people text or use the mobile Web?"

Dan laughed as he replied, "Sure, we can. We'll get to that later."

14

Sin Francisco

I rose from my bed and reached toward my dresser to silence the beeping alarm clock. As my fingers touched the wooden surface, I knocked a pile of papers and envelopes on the floor before finding the tiny lever. I lay back down and buried my face in the pillow. I did not need vision to know that I had just knocked to the carpet the pile of bills that never quite got any smaller. I was constantly reminded of my previous life while paying off bills from past vacations, shopping sprees, and home upgrades. I thought about all the people who hung around when I was sighted and no longer returned my calls. I could feel my tears moisten the satin sheets as I was embraced by loneliness. Even the city had turned its back on me as I got to know its blind side. My disenchantment grew every time I ran into buildings, doors, and people in public who could not see me blind.

I was seduced by San Francisco at the tender age of sixteen. I recall spending many nights on the Web, learning about the diverse architectures this well-engineered city had to offer. My eyes were fully engaged, refusing to blink as I took in the images of pastel-colored Victorians and breathtaking views of the bridge on the pixilated screen. Aside from all the beauty San Francisco had to offer, I also knew that it would be the only place I could live and feel safe as a gay male. The wave of gay bashings and the highly publicized killing of Matthew Shepard were reason enough to start creating a plan to get to "the city by the bay." I knew I had to get a job at one of the big-name companies in San Francisco's financial district, and I felt a college degree would be the ticket to get me hired.

I signed up for an SAT prep course and began to do research on colleges near San Francisco. In between reading university catalogs and school websites, I found my concentration interrupted by daydreams of living in a place with high tolerance for individuality. I figured that if someone could get away with wearing leather chaps in public every September, someone who was simply seeking to liberate himself from the claws of judgment would be a shoo-in.

A few days shy of my twenty-third birthday, my partner Jim, my cats, and I arrived in San Francisco's Richmond District. My first apartment overlooked Clement Street, and it felt surreal to have attained one of my childhood dreams. The city was more than I could have expected. Although I had frequently ventured into San Francisco on the weekends for festivities or outings to the Castro, I now could truly experience the day-to-day city life. The numerous cafés, restaurants, and cultural activities were all so familiar and welcoming to me. Perhaps, it was because I had envisioned my life on the enchanting seven-hilled city for so long.

I rose from my bed and slowly began to prepare for the day. Although I had begun to take classes at the LightHouse and knew of working blind people, I still questioned my ability to go back to work. A bigger doubt that haunted me was the fear of being unable to maintain a modest lifestyle in the city.

I was still scared of taking Muni and signed up with Mobility Plus, a service that gives disabled individuals rides to any destination in the city. My pickup window was approaching, and I decided to wait downstairs. My mom asked, "Do you want me to wait with you?"

I replied, "Nah, I got it. This stick is not so hard to use after all." It was the first time I felt someone smile, and it felt marvelous. I made my way down the winding set of steps that launched me in front of the Asian restaurant beneath my condo. I was received by a cold gust of wind that made my eyes water slightly. The Mobility Plus drivers knew I was blind and had to greet and identify themselves to me. This put me at ease and allowed me to just enjoy the commotion of Mission Street. I rolled my cane from left to right over a crack in the pavement as I was trying to figure out if the person a few steps behind me using the pay phone was a man or a woman, when suddenly I felt a hand over my face and then smelled a rosy perfume that arrived unannounced.

I then heard a woman's soft voice say, "God, please, bless his poor soul."

I took a step back before saying, "Who are you and what are you doing?!"

The woman answered, "You are blind because you are paying for your sins; I am helping you. Let me finish my blessing."

I replied, "I don't need your blessing! I was not born this way; I had an accident."

The woman asked, "Oh, what kind?"

I answered, "I was mugged in the Castro."

Her tone of voice changed before saying, "Ahh, He is giving you another chance. It's not too late to change your lifestyle around."

I was stunned. I had come to San Francisco to seek freedom from people's judgment, and I found it right outside my house. I could feel my eyes tearing as I said, "I believe in God, but not in your blessing. To me, blessing someone is like saying 'I love you.' You are only blessing me because you pity me. If you genuinely cared, you would have first said hello and asked how I was doing. If you really want to do me a favor, you can start by treating me like a person and not a charity."

I felt silence despite all the cars and people speeding by. I then heard, "Hi, Mr. Cipriani, it's Mobility Plus; I am your driver John."

I asked, "Is that woman still here?"

John replied, "Umm, there is a woman walking away at about five feet. Is everything okay?"

"Yup," I responded as I wiped the tears from my cheeks, grabbed his arm, and boarded the van.

In class, I told my classmates about my experience with the woman outside my house. I heard a few say, "I am sorry," coming from various corners of the room, but then it got silent.

Laurie Laroche, the LightHouse's social worker, chimed in and said, "People are funny about blindness. Some cultures see us as lost souls or bad luck, while in others, we are perceived as wise and valuable members of society."

Then, I heard an older woman say, "Well, I am not learning Braille!"

Another voice then said, "Oh, I need a talking scale. Do you guys sell those here, teacher?"

At twenty-seven, I was the youngest member of the class. Most of my classmates were seniors who had lost their sight from macular degeneration, a condition that slowly leads to blindness. I was consumed by loneliness, feeling misunderstood by my peers. Their concerns were acutely different from mine, and I knew it would take me too long to learn to be a blind person in this environment. After class, I talked to Laurie about my plans for reentering society and maybe even work. She began to tell me about the Orientation Center for the Blind (OCB) in Albany, California.

The words of the strange woman cloaked in rosy perfume would play in my head from time to time, but I transformed the frustration and anger it caused me into something positive. I knew the attempts I had previously made to re-acclimate were weak. I now had the motivation to develop and strive for a new set of goals.

15

Blind Bling

I felt the room begin to fill up and sensed someone sit next to me on the folding chair. It was my first blind conference, and I wanted to make sure I put my best foot forward, since I could possibly be networking with future employers. Instead of my usual jeans and hooded sweater, I opted for a pair of gray slacks and a black turtleneck. I figured if it works for Steve Jobs, it would work for me too. The man by my side began to talk to me, and I learned he was an engineer at Google. His success infused me with hope as I got details about his role for the Internet giant. I smiled to know I could apply at Google once my rehabilitation was complete. I spared the man any details of my assault or numerous surgeries and told him I was still in school. The blind community in the Bay Area is small and well-connected, and I did not want my cause of blindness to be my identifier.

A woman began to talk over a microphone, and the crowd instantly quieted down. We were all welcomed to the LightHouse and introduced to the tech companies presenting that day. Although I had yet to graduate from the LightHouse's basic skills course and was aware of my limited abilities with adaptive technology, I had grown tired of asking friends and family to do things for me. I also missed the modern conveniences of the Internet, texting, download-ing music, and GPS that were no longer within my reach. At times, it felt medieval to be unable to access or record information as simple as a phone number. Armed with two credit cards, I listened to the different presenters who, in excited voices, discussed their various devices. The theme of the conference was cell phones, and my throat became dry as my jaw repeatedly dropped in awe after hearing what each phone could do. The phone that stood out the most was one that used its camera to identify money or read labels on food or menus.

The hostess announced the conclusion of the presenta-tions, and I made my way toward the booths. I heard canes tapping and swishing in different directions and guide dogs jingle all around me. However, my thoughts remained on that phone that could change my life. With it, I would no longer have to ask people how much money I was holding or have them read restaurant menus to me.

A LightHouse staff member helped me find the booth I was seeking, and I began to speak to a cheery man. I held the tiny phone and gently caressed its smooth, slick design. I asked the man for the price as I dug into my pant pocket for my wallet. I almost dropped my cane when the guy said, "It's two grand for the phone, and it only works under this provider. Are you currently signed up with them?"

I tucked my wallet back in my pocket and took a giant step back as I answered, "No, I'm with another phone company."

I walked toward a group of voices nearby and stood quietly to eavesdrop. I began to listen to a woman say, "The talking application is three hundred dollars and can be downloaded to a phone. However, it only works with these phones that start at five hundred dollars." I knew she was talking about BlackBerries, which I realized were also currently outside my price range and decided to head toward the LightHouse store.

I asked the young woman to show me a few digital record-ers, and I was floored to realize the most basic one they had was three hundred and fifty dollars. I learned within a few minutes that color identifiers, barcode readers, and anything that could talk was priced out of my budget. I stepped aside and listened to men and women spend thousands on gadgets that made blindness tolerable, but sold as luxury items. My shoulders began to sink with disappointment as images of my sighted life flooded my thoughts. Before my eyes were broken, I made a good living and was never intimidated by flashy price tags. However, I now stood sightless and sticker shocked over blind equipment. I was brought back to the present by a tall person running into me. A man excused himself, and I asked my surroundings, "Why is everything for the blind so expensive?"

A woman on my left replied, "That's because we are not the intended customer."

The tall man chimed in with, "That's absolutely right; it's the government these companies want to sell to."

Within a few minutes, I learned that these companies had no intention to sell these items to me, because they could get more money elsewhere. Many of the people buying items that day had saved for months, so they could afford their purchases. The woman asked me, "Are you still with rehab?"

I explained that I had only been working with the Light-House for a short time, but that I was to start at the OCB very soon.

The man interjected with, "Good, you should have your rehab counselor buy your stuff while you are in training. Cuz, once they close your case, it will be all up to you."

I bit my lower lip and gave a shaky, "Oh, okay."

My ears still stinging with the sounds of the high cost of my new life, I turned to inquire about talking watches. The clerk brought out a few designs with choices of silver, gold, and leather bands. I gently touched each watch as I played with the buttons and heard the range in phonics voices. I was grossed out by the stiff leather band, which felt more like plastic. I was listening to the sad robotic voice deliver the time when the clerk added, "That one is forty-five dollars."

I asked the woman, "Is this real silver? You can fool my eyes but not my skin." The woman confirmed its authenticity, and I laughed before saying, "Good, my wrist would itch and turn green in anger." I made my purchase and headed out to the lobby to await my ride. I thought about my future blind investments as I caressed my first piece of blind bling.

16

The School for Misfit Toys

My mom came out of her room and said, "There is a little bus outside; I think that's your ride."

I remained quiet as I struggled to peel myself from the couch and unfold my cane.

I reached out for my luggage with my free hand and felt my sister's fingers on my arm as she whispered, "I'll take the gray one down for you."

I heard the small set of wheels rattle their way out my condo and fade down the stairs. My mom patted my back and said, "Let's go!"

I could feel the anxiety build in my chest as I made my way out my building. "Cipriani!" shouted a deep voice from a few feet away.

I gave out a short, "Right here!" as I felt my sister's arms reach around me for a hug.

She softly said, "He knows; he is already putting your stuff in the bus."

I let out a shaky "okay" and felt my mom hold my other arm. I could now feel the anxiety burn around my collarbone and bit my tongue to keep myself from tearing. I broke my family's embrace by saying, "I'll be back to visit in a few weeks."

I boarded the vehicle and attempted to push all my anxiety and self-doubt aside. I sensed the bus start to speed up and knew we had entered the freeway. I shifted my thoughts to the blind school and convinced myself it would be just as fun and exciting as when I moved into the dorms at Notre Dame de Namur University. I was intrigued by the idea of having a blind roommate and chuckled when I realized that we could still have privacy even in front of each other because of our lack of sight. I smiled and enjoyed the cool, crisp air stroking my face and hair.

"We're here," said the driver. I pulled out my cane and stepped off the bus. I heard the driver place my luggage next to me as he asked me to wait while he went to find someone.

From a distance, I heard a woman say, "Hi, Belo." She walked up to me and gently escorted me to the main office. I felt a faint breeze shoot behind a set of opening automatic doors. She sat me down on a soft leather couch and informed me that a staff member would take my stuff to the dorms. I heard the automatic doors open again, and the room suddenly became overtaken by canes tapping and swishing over the tiled floor.

"Who's in front of me?"

"It's Polly; who's that?"

"It's Aina; I think we're in the lobby. You went the wrong way."

They both began to chuckle, and my laugh soon joined theirs. Polly had a very distinctive voice. It was probably the most unique and memorable set of vocal cords I had listened to since I had lost my sight. It was a combination of Macy Gray and an old southern belle.

"Who's there on the couch?" asked Polly.

I was shocked she was able to point out my location. I

answered timidly, "I'm Belo." I extended my hand out like I had become accustomed to at the LightHouse and reached out into the air.

"Do you have any vision?" asked Aina.

"Nope, nothing at all," I shyly answered as I retracted my neglected hand. "Oh, me neither," replied Aina.

They pitter-pattered out of the lobby through a door on the opposite side of the room. I took a deep breath and sunk back into the sofa. I heard a cane gently glide over the floor, a marked contrast from the women who had just left, and a cheery man shouted, "Hi, Belo!" He sat next to me and firmly shook my hand. "Now, Belo, a mobility instructor will be with you in a few minutes to give you a tour of the school and have you meet some of your teachers. Someone will record your schedule on tape, hopefully by tomorrow. Can you see shadows or movement?"

"No, it's all black," I replied. After being at the Light-House for a couple of months, I had come to terms with the sight questions. I accepted the fact that the Orientation Center for the Blind would be similar in that regard.

A young voice surfaced from across the room and said, "Hi, Belo. I'm Betty. I will be doing some mobility with you until your schedule gets recorded." Betty walked me around campus and pointed out unusual landmarks. "Do you feel this metal plate with your cane?" I nodded and she continued, "Well, when you feel the metal surface, you need to start turning left toward the cafeteria."

I was so excited to learn that the school had such a simple layout and that it was built to be a blind teaching facility. Everything was accessible and made sense from a blind perspective. Every entrance had a doormat and automatic doors. The school was made up of buildings that formed a big square, which made it simple to get from one structure to the next. Betty walked me through the gym and said, "You will be meeting here for PE class."

I laughed out loud and said, "PE? I haven't heard that expression since high school."

Betty took a few steps toward me on the rubber floor and said, "It's not high school, but you will be learning to do everything again. Let's go to your room; I am sure your stuff is there by now."

We went up a set of stairs and took a few steps. Betty placed my hand over a keypad and said, "You're in room nine; I'll give you your password." The door made a low beeping sound, and I pulled the door handle. "Your bed is on the right side, Belo. The bathroom is on the left wall. Your bathroom mate is Jose."

"Bathroom mate? Is that my roommate?" I asked.

"No, there are four people to every bathroom. Jose's roommate just graduated, and Kyle, who was staying in this room, died a week ago," answered Betty.

My stomach knotted, and I asked, "He died here?"

"No, no, he was back at home. Your teacher will talk about it today in your Blind Law class." Betty told me she would be back later to check on me and that I had the rest of the morning free. I heard her feet shuffle out the room as I slowly collapsed onto the firm mattress. I was curious to know how Kyle died and began to weave possible scenarios in my mind. I thought that maybe he was hit by a car while crossing a street by himself, or perhaps he took the wrong medicine because he mixed up bottles somehow. I felt goose bumps and sat up to take a few breaths. I then shocked myself when I conceived a new concern. I wondered if I was more susceptible to paranormal activity now that I was blind. I couldn't see ghosts when I was sighted, but maybe I could sense them now. I jumped off the bed and made my way to the TV room downstairs.

I was counting my steps, hoping not to get lost when I heard a brittle voice say, "Hi, I'm Rose. You must be the new guy."

I smiled and said, "Yeah, I'm Belo." The woman helped me find a seat in the TV room and began to tell me about herself. I learned that she had some vision but that she had been blind for her whole life.

"Yup, I was a total, and one day I could see. My doctors have no explanation," continued Rose. I told her I was assaulted a year prior and that I was still dealing with court hearings and attorneys. I purposely left out the fact that the defendants in my civil case were at one point like family and that their betrayal still burned twelve months later. Rose seemed unaffected by my story and began to tell me about her disease. "I have sickle-cell anemia," Rose said as she went over frightening details about her weekly dialysis process.

A deep voice shouted unexpectedly, "Who dat?! Is this the TV room?!"

Rose helped the guy find a seat as well and said, "Belo, this is Eric." Eric began to tell me about the bullet that entered through the back of his head and exited through his face, disintegrating his eye. He had arrived a week before and told me that he was thankful to be around people who understood him. We bonded over stories about surgeries, detectives, and being totally blind. "I feel ya, brotha!" Eric said. All of our talking watches went off at the same time, announcing the noon hour, and we all chuckled as we headed toward the cafeteria.

The energy in the cafeteria was vibrant and bursting with laughter from what appeared to be every corner of the room. The ambiance seemed so positive and uplifting compared to my experience at the LightHouse. I was instructed to grab a tray by a woman behind me in line. I placed myself along a metal table where I was able to smell warm pasta and cooked vegetables. "We got spaghetti and salad. Do you want both, son?" asked a raspy voice.

I nodded and began to worry when I realized I had to carry my tray with food and use my cane at the same time. The man behind me told me to grab my tray with the left hand and cane with the right. I did as I was told and heard a woman say, "Do you want to sit with us? I'm Norah, by the way." She helped me find a seat and introduced me to the people sitting around us. I quickly learned that everyone sitting around me was a total with the exception of Norah.

As we were talking, I felt a hand on my shoulder and realized it was Betty telling me she was going to walk me to meet some of my teachers and have some basic assessments done. Betty explained the layout of the building where most of my classes would take place. "This is called the bottom of the T, Belo," Betty said and continued to tell me that the hallway was in the shape of the letter T. She introduced me to the computer teacher and left the room.

"I'm sorry; I already forgot your name. I have been learning so many new voices and names," I admitted in a confused tone.

"I'm Valentina, Belo, and I'm very happy you're here." I heard her heels click on the floor as she walked around the classroom. There was something different about her voice, but I was unable to figure out what. She began to ask about my technical skills and if I had done any training with JAWS (Job Access with Speech) at the LightHouse. I told her that I knew that JAWS was a screen reader that worked with Windows, but that I only played with it once at the Light-House. We had only been talking for about twenty minutes or so, but Valentina made me feel at ease. "All your concerns about work are very valid, Belo, but you seem fairly technical, and I think you will learn JAWS with no problems," Valentina said.

Feeling a little calmer, I switched the topic with, "How can I feel safe traveling on my own though? I am not sure if there is a solution to that problem." Valentina began to tell me she was transgendered and had been mugged outside her apartment. "Is that how you lost your sight?" I asked in a terrified manner.

"Oh no, I lost my sight from Retinitis Pigmentosa, but someone took advantage of my blindness." She told me for months she was afraid to leave her house, but that she had recently found hope.

I was eager to know how Valentina was able to overcome such a tragic experience and curiously asked, "What did you do to find hope?"

I sensed her sit on a chair next to me, and she said, "I'm getting a guide dog; I'll be going to Guide Dogs for the Blind this summer." For the first time in my blind life, I allowed my mind to consider the possibility of using a dog.

Betty's voice surfaced with a brisk hello, and we headed toward the Blind Law classroom. She helped me find a chair and introduced me to more students. I noticed everyone kept announcing their names as they entered the room. The class began with the instructor asking me to introduce myself to the entire group. In the format of an AA meeting, I greeted the other students, "Hi, I'm Belo, and I'm a total."

In unison, the choir of voices said, "Hi, Belo, welcome to OCB!"

17

Mosaic

I arrived at my room after my first of what would be many rowdy dinners at OCB and was greeted by a pungent odor. I pulled out a bottle of air freshener from one of my bags and began to defend my room from the stench. I realized the smell was coming from the bathroom and immediately closed and locked the door. I sprayed my room a few more times and recalled a fact I learned at the LightHouse. Dan once told me that 80 percent of the way in which the brain takes in data is visual and that once the sight is gone, the other senses will try to compensate. He also mentioned that all blind people adapt and learn to harness their other senses differently. I eagerly waited for the day I could pick up sounds from distant places, but my bionic hearing never came. Instead, it was my senses of smell and taste that woke from their slumber. My nose rejected the citrus undertones of my favorite cologne, forcing me to switch to musky and more subtle fragrances. My tongue disapproved of all my comfort foods and now found Asian and Indian spices dangerously enticing.

I basked in the vanilla oasis I'd just created and began to unpack my bags. I found a chip on the rim of my Gemini coffee cup and contemplated throwing it away, but figured I could use it to store change and shoved it into a drawer.

I knew of sophisticated labeling techniques using Braille and other blind tools; however, since I still remained illiterate, I was obliged to use primitive techniques like rubber bands and bump dots. I smiled and mentally thanked my two younger sisters who had taught me various ways of tying and braiding rubber bands to create Chinese jump ropes, a popular jumping game for girls in the 1980s. I carefully formed knots on bands that hugged glass bottles or plastic containers, curling my lip as I acknowledged the hours it was taking me to get settled. Although I understood it was unfair to contrast my blind to my sighted self, I also knew it was unrealistic for me not to do so. I was halfway done putting my clothes into the wooden cabinets, when I became restless and decided to stick the rest of my shirts and pants into any drawer. I figured most of the students couldn't see me anyway, and the ones who had any vision should just understand.

I dove onto my bed and got lost in the fresh laundry aroma coming from my clothes and sheets. In what seemed like only a few moments, I heard a knock on the door. I opened my eyes and saw the yellow oak door open. A woman resembling Angelina Jolie walked in, her chestnut hair caught in a gust of wind, she smiled before asking, "How is everything, Belo?" The minute I heard her voice I realized it was Betty. I was suddenly dressed in a white turtleneck, gray slacks, and shiny black shoes. I took a step toward Betty and saw her turn into Barbara Walters. She gave me a hug and said, "It's Norah, by the way." I heard a howling from my bathroom and watched Norah morph into my Capoiera Master. I was suddenly scared by his dark brown eyes that looked back at me with deep disappointment. "Come on, get in there and fight!" he shouted. I stood facing a metal door covered with odd-looking carvings. I was now wearing my Capoiera uniform: white tank, Lycra baggy pants, and my blue and yellow cord that wrapped around my waist. The room began to look fuzzy and then went all dark.

I heard the howling again and sat up immediately. I shifted my body toward the other bed on the opposite wall and then heard the creepy cry come from my bathroom. I took a few deep breaths and heard the doorknob fiercely move back and forth, slightly shaking the wooden door. I felt my chest beat faster and picked up the echolike words coming from the next room, "Let me in! Let me in!" cried the male voice. I lay back down wishing that by ignoring the sounds, I could somehow make them go away. I felt foreign to myself. When I was sighted, I was never afraid of weird noises or of being alone. I now lay in a small bed, frozen in fear, and unable to think logically. I suddenly heard the voice become frustrated and swear in Spanish. I slithered out of bed and cautiously walked to the bathroom. The Spanish continued, and I assumed it was my bathroom mate Jose, who I had yet to meet.

"Is that you, Jose?" I asked in a shaky tone.

"Oh yeah, where am I?" Jose inquired.

I told him he was in the bathroom and that he had to face the other direction and find the opposing door.

He began to whistle and asked, "Can you please open the door?" I quickly went from being startled to annoyed.

I assumed Jose was drunk and said to him, "Go to the other door; that's your room."

I heard him drag his cane and run into the shower door. I visualized the layout of the bathroom in my mind and walked inside. I could sense Jose against the sink and said, "Come this way." I found the doorknob with my right hand and tapped on the door with an open palm.

Jose remained quiet as I could hear his fingers trail the

cold tiled wall. He entered his room and said, "Thanks, Kyle, see you tomorrow."

I could tell there was more than blindness limiting him. The alarm on my wrist watch went off, and someone began to knock on my door. I heard Betty's voice and began to move my head in various directions, blinking profusely as I silenced the fake rooster. Everything stayed black, and I confirmed I was awake and gingerly answered the door. Betty handed me my class schedule in the shape of a cassette tape as she inquired about my first night at the dorms. I brought up my encounter with Jose, and she told me Jose, like others in the group, survived major head trauma but that she could not go into any details with me. I nodded my head as Betty's words made me feel grateful that the trauma to my head left my motor skills intact and told Betty I needed to get dressed.

Back in my dorm, I slowly walked toward the tape player that had come with the room. I said aloud in a comical tone, "This is so '80s," as I jammed the cassette into the player and experimented with the buttons. An older woman's voice filled the room as her bored tone went over my schedule. To my surprise, it varied drastically from day to day, making it overwhelming to try to memorize it. I focused just on the classes for the day and recited the course names as I wrestled a sweater on and headed to class.

I walked into a stuffy room and asked, "Is this Daily Living Skills?"

A perky and energetic voice pierced my right ear. "Hi there! You must be Belo; I'm Carmen." Carmen elaborated on the goals for the class as she walked me through different stations that simulated diverse home environments. "Do you do any cleaning around your home?" Carmen inquired.

Her question fueled my mind with images of vacuuming my cat's hair off the area rug in my study and scrubbing my claw foot tub using baking soda. I turned my head toward her voice and said, "No, not since I lost it all."

I gave up trying to remember everyone's name and voice and simply listened to the vignettes that bounced from every wall and window in the school. Over the course of the day, I learned that there were three headshot-wound victims, four people who were blind from birth but only recently independent, and multiple cases of diabetes-related vision loss. I skipped dinner and spent the next couple hours in my dorm trying to understand tragedies and why they occur to certain people. I heard laughter come from the kitchenette outside my room and made my way toward the giggling. A young guy shouted, "Quit or I'm gonna kick your ass!"

A bubbly girl replied, "Not if you can't find me." The laughter suddenly stopped and the girl asked, "Who's there?"

I mumbled, "Um, I'm Belo. I was gonna make some tea."

I quickly learned that Tessa and William had been there for a few months and that they hung out frequently at bars, clubs, theaters, and even bowling alleys. "So, can I help you make that tea?" asked Tessa. I accepted her offer and went to my room to fetch my Gemini cup. I felt the chip on the rim and paused for a second. A sense of strength came over me, and I accepted the fact that I was broken, yet not shattered. I just have to drink from the other side I thought and joined the laughter.

18

Pucker Up!

I could not stop yawning in Daily Living Skills, and Carmen asked, "Long night, Belo?"

I smiled while attempting to thread a needle. "Um, I made friends with people in the dorms and stayed up pretty late talking. It's so refreshing to be around so many blind people."

Carmen handed me a small tray with an eraser on it and explained that all my projects would go on the tray. She added, "Half of the learning happens in class, and the rest happens in the dorms."

I never learned to sew, and it felt medieval to have it be part of my training. However, after speaking with Tessa and the gang, I realized this is where they all started. Pulling the thread through, I sat up from my chair and exclaimed, "I did it, Carmen! Now I can get married!" Carmen and I both laughed hysterically, and she excused me for lunch.

I was walking very slowly, counting the doors with my left hand and caning with the other, when I heard Tessa's bubbly shout, "Oh, there you are, Belo! I've been looking for you. Grab my arm; let's go to lunch." She helped me with my food tray and sat me next to Megean and Nelson.

As I bit into my burger, I felt a piece of lettuce drop from my lunch and fall onto my shirt. I shouted. "Crap, now I'm a mess."

They all laughed and Nelson said, "Don't trip. We all are. I'm gonna change my shirt after I eat."

Megean rubbed my shoulder and said, "Me too. I got dressing on my pants." We all laughed as I picked the food off my shirt. Eating with my sighted friends and family had become stressful. I worried every time I spilled or knocked something off the table. They quickly cleaned it up for me and repeated over and over that it was okay. Yet, it didn't feel okay, because it was so frustrating to have to concentrate so hard to enjoy a meal. Now I could forget about eating things incorrectly and enjoy the food. Tessa asked me if I wanted to go to the store with them, and I happily accepted.

We all prepared for the trip to Long's Drugstore by arming ourselves with baseball caps to alert us if we are going to hit something with our face, sunglasses to keep things from flying into our eyes, and spare canes for backup. I was so blown away with how synchronized we all were. We lined up and selected Tessa to guide us, since she had the most vision and the strongest cane technique. I was placed in the middle of the line so that I would not veer off course and get lost. I focused on the swishing and tapping that came from ahead of me to keep my bearings. Tessa would call out driveways, garbage bins, and anything else we could run into, "There is a shopping cart on the left."

We lined up to cross San Pablo Street, and although I had often heard the bird noises at street crossings when I was sighted, now for the first time, I listened for the chirping. I asked, "Um, do we cross now? It doesn't sound like a chirp." Tessa explained that crossing from north to south was a beeping noise, and crossing west to east was the bird.

I responded, "Oh, so that means we're still waiting."

Tessa told me I was picking things up quickly and gave me a hug. The mechanical bird started to sing, and we all proceeded across. San Pablo Street is very wide, and I grew fearful, since I could feel the cars on my right just inches away. Their engines sounded like bulls breathing viciously as they waited to attack, pushing me to walk faster.

I heard automatic doors open and felt the air-conditioned breeze stroke my face. A clerk greeted the group and helped us navigate the store. Megean and I were bringing up the rear, struggling to hear Nelson and Tessa talking to the clerk. I shuffled my feet toward Tessa's voice and inquired, "So, what are we getting from here?"

Nelson replied nonchalantly, "Condoms and liquor."

I laughed and Tessa chimed in, "Just because we're blind doesn't mean we can't play." Memories of the first day I hung out with the brothers and Jesus flooded my thoughts. Did I somehow end up hanging out with the "bad crowd" at OCB? I remained quiet while the clerk went over the different types of condoms, and Nelson made a selection. I knew drinking and sex were not allowed in the dorms, but I bit my tongue and followed everyone to the liquor aisle. Tessa and Nelson went back and forth on what to drink as the clerk read over the liquors.

The last couple of months were spent mainly in bed, healing physically and spiritually. I had forgotten how good it felt to have fun and decided to take the plunge. "I used to be a bartender. I can make you guys anything." The group gasped, and I even heard some clapping. I suggested a few drinks, and we unanimously decided on apple martinis.

Back on campus, we headed back to our respective rooms and promised to meet in Megean and Tessa's room at 10:00 PM. I got the urge to dress up and was excited to find one of my old AX clubbing shirts in my closet. My hair had gotten pretty long, and I decided to rock an Afro. I picked at my curls for a few minutes and sprayed on some cologne. I decided to take my docking station and iPod with me and quietly walked to room 18.

I knocked on the door and whispered, "It's Belo." Tessa gingerly opened the door and pulled me inside. I heard heels on the floor and asked, "Tessa, are you dressed up?"

The group giggled, and a new voice answered, "We all are. It feels good too. I'm Lily."

I remembered she had given me my tour a few months back and said, "Oh, I know you! Glad you're here." I plugged in my docking station and played 2Pac. I heard Nelson's voice and figured out he was sitting next to Lily. Soon, I heard them kissing. I realized who the condoms were for and smiled. I set up the bar and started to make drinks.

Lily asked, "So, what's in an apple martini?"

Shaking a cup of ice as I poured liquor, I answered, "Vodka and Apple Pucker, lots of Pucker."

I heard William's voice ask me for a drink, and I was slightly startled because I didn't know he was in the room. He took the cup from my hand and asked, "Belo, are you white?" I laughed and told the group that my family was Brazilian on my dad's side and Jewish Italian on my mom's. I mentioned that my mom grew up in Central and South America, which is why I could speak Spanish and Portuguese.

"I'm pretty brown with big, curly hair," I added. I walked around the room and let everyone touch my hair.

Megean and Nelson both gasped while they ran their fingers through my curls. "Oh shit, dude! You got a fro!" Nelson shouted.

They all had made guesses, but William had the best guess. "I knew you had some Italian in you," he exclaimed.

We all shared our vision-loss stories. I was soon wiping

tears from my face, while I poured drinks. William was born blind and shared how he was teased growing up and even abandoned in a field by some mean kids. Tessa and Megean both lost their sight from retinitis pigmentosa, so their visual loss was slow and painful. Lily was one of the many diabetic cases at OCB and lost her sight within a few weeks. Nelson had been shot in the head, and I wanted to scream so bad when I touched the indentation on the side of his skull. The broken bone felt like a baby's soft spot, and it made me angry. I saved my story for last on purpose, because I was unsure of how much to share with this new group of friends. After hearing everyone's sad truth, I decided to open up completely and not spare any detail. It was the first time since the assault that I had been so honest. Purging myself felt therapeutic. I was pleased with their reactions, and I found them deeply comforting. There were no hollow apologies from any of them.

William said, "Dude, you have every right to be pissed off."

I cried for a few seconds, and Tessa said, "It's okay to hate them, Belo. Hating them does *not* make you a bad person."

I refreshed the group's drinks and suggested a toast. "Cheers to being blind and alive!" I said.

19

Quack!

I was concentrating on finding the computer classroom and mentally cheered *yes!* when I felt the tiled floor turn into carpet with the tip of my cane. I heard a weird sound coming from Valentina's office that sounded like a VCR chewing up a tape. I found an empty chair and made myself comfortable as I cued my cassette recorder to take notes. Valentina came out of her office and, without making any sound, took a seat next to me, startling me as she said, "Morning, Belo. Let's get to work."

I was amazed with how she moved around without a cane, avoiding furniture and holding a conversation simultaneously. I asked her, "How do you do that? It's like you can see or something."

Valentina laughed and told me that she had been working at OCB long enough to have a mental map of the classroom. "It takes time, Belo, but you'll get there," she added.

I hit the record button as I told Valentina that I could not believe I was using a tape recorder. "It feels like a World War II walkie-talkie." We both laughed, and she began her class.

She really made a point to emphasize the importance of mastering JAWS and the numerous ways it would impact my blind life. "It will make you more independent, because you'll be able to order food and buy clothes or bulky items online that are hard for blind people to move and carry," Valentina continued.

I was fortunate to have attended a high school that made typing a requirement for graduation. I felt fairly familiar with the layout of the keyboard, and Valentina moved me right into basic JAWS commands. The flat, robotic voice read back the words I had typed and I asked, "Why is the computer saying 'quack?'"

She responded, "It's not saying 'quack.' It's saying 'blank.' That means you are on an edit field, and you can start typing." I had Valentina slow the speak and spell style voice down to the slowest setting possible. I then heard that same weird tape-chewing noise from earlier, and Valentina said, "Oh, my download is complete." I was shocked to realize that the gibberish from earlier was her JAWS setting, which in no way resembled real speech.

A half an hour later, I began to feel pain around my temple and eyebrows. The level of concentration JAWS required to understand was quickly making me tired. I asked Valentina if I could take a break, and she said, "Don't push yourself too hard, Belo; this is all very difficult stuff to learn." I wrapped my arms around my head on the table and heard Valentina working on her computer from a distance. It was deeply stressful to struggle with something that was vital to my survival. I knew I had to learn JAWS if I ever wanted to get a job, go to school, or buy food. The alarm on a nearby desk went off, and it was time to go to my next class.

The Prevocational Class was aimed at introducing students to blind technology for work and school purposes. Meili Wu had a thick Chinese accent and was very excited to teach all of us. She was an alumnus from OCB and understood the stress associated with trying to pick up a bunch of new skills at the same time. She was having me test different digital recorders and PDAs when I told her, "I am really tired of all these robotic voices."

I heard her walk toward me and take a seat on a nearby chair. She asked, "Am I giving you too much, Belo?"

I impulsively shook my head *no*; then, I remembered she was a total as well and replied, "It just feels so sci-fi, you know? Blindness is so isolating, and on top of all that, we depend on artificial voices to survive."

Meili said, "I know what you mean, Belo. If my devices ever break down and die, I feel like I'll die too."

I am not sure if it was her accent or how dramatic she sounded when she said "die," but I began to chuckle. She told me that adaptive technology had greatly advanced in the last ten years, but as a backup, I should learn to also perform tasks without technology. Meili added that she used to be a photojournalist before she lost her sight. Without any concern about sounding rude, I asked for her story. I was terrified to learn that her vision loss was caused by an allergic reaction to medication. I asked myself mentally, *Who does she blame for her blindness? God? The world? Science?*

I thought about the challenge of not having a person or group of people to blame for my blindness. At times, it was easier to focus my anger and frustration at Carlos to push myself to move forward with life. Although childish, it is natural and human to blame others for one's misfortunes. I found channeling my anger at my attackers kept me from falling apart. However, over the past few days, I had met people who lost their sight through disease, which I imagined was harder to deal with. Many of my diabetic friends who had neuropathy on their fingers and were unable to read Braille blamed themselves for their misfortune. I often heard remorse and regret for their past negligence with their diet and medication. Without access to Braille, many of the diabetics had limited options in blind technology, reducing their resources to very few.

I realized after talking to Meili that I had options and let that idea bounce in my head as the quacking continued throughout the rest of the day. While using a talking microwave in cooking class, I thought about the day that the quacks would fly away and leave behind clear voices.

20

Lap Dance

I was sitting on one of the three benches in the school's quad, where every hour a different group of students waited for a mobility instructor to assign a route. Norah and I were discussing Braille class, when I heard my teacher, Bob, say, "Okay, Belo! Today you will be riding the bus on your own."

I gave out a comical "what!" similar to the "what" heard in any song featuring the artist Lil Jon. I reluctantly peeled myself off the bench and dragged my feet toward San Pablo Street. I had ridden the bus with mobility staff before but never on my own. It was nerve-racking, but at the same time exciting, since I knew it was a rite of passage every student at OCB must face.

I reached the bus stop where the aroma from the nearby coffee shop greeted me and alerted me of my location. Bob slipped a laminated card into my hand that felt similar to a driver's license. I asked, "Is this a fancy bus pass?"

His hardy Santa Claus chuckle quickly filled the bus shelter as I paused for an answer. Bob replied, "It says the following: 'Hi, my name is Belo Cipriani, and I am a student at OCB. If you find me, please contact the number below.'"

Feeling like a house pet, I jammed the card into my shorts. I heard the bus approaching and felt my stomach knotting. The double doors shot out a small gust of wind, and I realized it was too late to back out. I tapped my cane up the steps and found a metal box where I dropped a few coins. Bob shouted from behind me, "Get off on Solano," and the bus began to move.

The driver did not say anything to me, and, annoyed, I began to look for a seat with my white stick. Believing I had located an empty spot, I smiled and began to move toward the tip of my cane and immediately sat. I felt a knee on the back of my leg and jumped up. I responded dramatically, "Oh crap! I'm really sorry." I heard no response at all, even though I could hear something breathing on the chair. I pulled toward the seats on the opposite side, this time using my hand to look for a space. I felt soft fabric and was stunned to realize I was *brailling* another leg inappropriately. Luckily, I found a metal pole with my other hand and wrapped my body around it. I swallowed before shouting, "I guess I'm giving out lap dances today!" I heard a phonics voice similar to the one on my talking watch announce my stop, and I cautiously exited the bus and met up with Bob.

Back at school, pandemonium exploded among my classmates when I told them about my Moulin Rouge escapade. We laughed for eons. It became a standing joke at the OCB. When one of us newly blind students entered the classroom, we would laughingly call out, "Is there somewhere for me to sit, or am I giving out lap dances today?"

A few days later, I was reviewing the sets of dots that I was learning to decipher, and I sunk into a plush, velvet sofa in a nearby café. I heard a man's voice call out, "Could someone help me?"

I ignored him, assuming mine was not the help he sought, and put my headphones on. A few seconds afterward, I felt human weight on my lap. I jumped and heard myself react abruptly, "What the hell?!"

The male voice from a moment ago responded, "Sorry! I'm blind."

Surprised, I said, "Oh ... me too."

We both chuckled, and I moved my bags to make room for him on the couch. When he sat near me, I realized he was old and fragile. I asked if I could get him something. "Coffee, please," he replied.

His grateful response infused me with confidence. Leaving my cane, I took the few measured steps to the counter and ordered his drink. As I unfolded the marked bills from my wallet, I realized that I could help after all.

21

Braille Jail

Braille was something I found aesthetically pleasing when I was sighted. The beautiful bumps that appeared on the McDonald's soft drink lids and on signs seemed like ancient hieroglyphs to me. During my short interaction with the LightHouse, I had a brief introduction course in Braille that sparked my interest in the tactile symbols. When I was given my first alphabet card, I knew it would be a rigorous journey back to literacy as I glided my fingers over the bumps that reminded me of the popcorn ceiling I had in my room as a kid. When I arrived at OCB, I found the support of my classmates who were all struggling with the raised dots as well. Rob Sterling, my Braille teacher, had the deepest voice I had ever heard. It was no surprise when I learned that he was a radio DJ and a musician on the side. His lessons were all memorable, as if I were being taught by Scar from *The Lion King*. Rob was always pleasant, yet his voice was fairly hard to shake off and occasionally left my ears ringing.

There are two levels to the letters for the blind. Grade One Braille focuses just on the letters from the alphabet, which I learned to decipher in a few weeks. It was learning the Grade Two Braille that made my fingers tremble with frustration. Braille takes up more room on a page than regular text and is, therefore, contracted to spare room, yet Braille texts are still heavy and bulky. Some symbols have multiple meanings, making it confusing for someone who was previously only concerned with twenty-six letters.

Aside from saturating my brain with over one hundred contracted Braille signs, I was also struggling with figuring out which hand and fingers to read with. I went back and forth between my left and right index finger, and with no luck, I even gave my pinkies a try. Although I picked up new Braille signs almost weekly, I would struggle with menus at restaurants, causing a love–hate relationship between me and the raised bumps. It was deeply annoying when friends, family, and strangers on the street would ask if I had learned Braille. I wondered why they never asked about anything else like mobility or how I groomed myself. Everyone wanted to know if I had Braille keys, Braille scissors, or even a Braille comb. I could hear the undertones of surprise in the voices when I revealed that, aside from Braille books and labels for movies or food, I simply used the same things they had at home.

I was wrapping up a mobility lesson and awaited the bus on University Avenue in Berkeley when I sensed someone sit next to me. A woman said, "Hello, I'm Lydia. How are you?"

Unsure if the young woman was addressing me, I timidly replied, "Um, I'm Belo, and I'm doing okay."

The bus shelter became filled with rumbling sounds coming from a motorcycle a few feet away. Then, the girl asked, "Can you read Braille?" I rolled my eyes behind my dark-tinted shades and nodded yes twice.

I heard the unfolding of a plastic bag as Lydia said, "I bought this Braille card for my boyfriend, but I want to make sure of what it says."

I uncurled my lip and smiled as I envisioned myself in a

relationship someday. This guy might have been blind, but that did not stop him from seizing the attention of a sweet girl. She placed the card in my hands, and I prayed the bumps were all symbols I knew. I gently caressed the card as I translated the simple birthday message. She cheered, "Very cool." I reached into my bag and took out my Slate and Stylist from a small pouch. Lydia asked, "What's that?"

I told her it was a portable Braille sketcher and said, "All this card is missing is your name; let me write it for you."

Lydia gasped and thanked me profusely. Luckily, her name did not have any contractions, and in a few seconds, I carved her name on the soft cardboard. Lydia and I said our goodbyes and boarded different busses.

I arrived back at OCB, eagerly anticipating my Braille class. I whistled down the hallway and into Rob's class and heard other students wrestling paper and hitting the keys on the Braille writers. Rob had some vision and roared, "Welcome to the Braille Jail, Belo. There is a chair on your right." I thought about his comment and flashed a smile, since I could finally imagine myself completing my sentence and rejoining the world.

22

Super Blind

After being at the OCB for a few weeks, I began to recognize the various types of people that exist within the blind world. There were the whiners, who used their blindness as an excuse to get out of doing anything themselves—a crowd that I was a member of during the months following the assault. Many of the whiners had been enabled and spoiled by their families, keeping them from maturing as capable members of society. There was the fun crowd that seemed unaffected by their vision loss and planned to live off social security for the rest of their lives. These were the folks who spent their entire federal checks on alcohol, weed, and junk that ended up under their beds unused. They eagerly waited the first of every month to splurge all over again. The class of blind people that most sighted individuals seem to be familiar with is a category I refer to as "Super Blind." This cohort consists of Helen Keller, the guy that climbed Mt. Everest, and the comic book superhero Daredevil. The "Super Blind" make it challenging sometimes for one to mingle with the visual community, because people expect those abilities from the rest of the blind family. At one point, I even had some guy at the bus stop ask me if I could hear his heartbeat. He figured I could listen to it standing two feet from him.

The group of blind people I eagerly wanted to belong to was the working class. Only about 30 percent of working-age blind persons are employed, a number I found both discouraging and hopeful. I figured 30 percent is better than zero and allowed that to be my inspiration to continue through my rehabilitation.

Norah, Lily, and I were passing time in the TV room between classes when Lily brought up Tessa. "So, Belo, what are we doing for Tessa's graduation?" she asked.

Norah sighed before saying, "I'm sure she'll be quite happy at the bar."

Lily and I ignored Norah's comment, and I began to tell her about the JAWS class I signed up for at the LightHouse that Saturday. "If we're doing anything for Tessa, it's gonna have to be on Friday," I added.

"I am spending Saturday with my son, so we should let Tessa know we should plan for Friday," Lily retorted.

Norah said, "Aww, what are you and your son doing, Lily?"

Lily giggled before answering, "We're watching *The Eye.*"

"I hate that movie!" I shouted and went over the details of the film I found annoying. I explained to both of them how frustrating it had become to encounter these unrealistic representations of the blind in the media. "I am tired of the blind musician, blind witch, or blind people with supernatural abilities," I added in an agitated tone.

Lily laughed and asked, "What does all that have to do with *The Eye*? I thought it's about a girl who gets her sight back."

I told Lily she was right, but that I was bothered by the

fact they had made the girl "Super Blind" during her blind phase. Norah chimed in with, "I know what you mean, Belo, and it ticks me off too. We should all start making capes in sewing class."

We all began to chuckle, and Lily inquired, "So, what makes this chick 'Super Blind?'"

I explained to them that the protagonist was, no surprise, a violinist and that the movie starts with her saving a sighted guy from getting hit by a bus. I heard my mobility instructor call my name from a distance, and I unfolded my cane. Before exiting the room I said, "Okay, let's see how many sighted people I save during my mobility lesson," and laughed as I thought how absurd the whole thing sounded.

Although the OCB curriculum consisted of a few JAWS and other blind technology classes per week, I strongly believed that taking additional lessons on the weekend through the LightHouse would accelerate my training. It was always difficult to skip social functions with my blind friends, since I knew that I would have very limited opportunities in the future to be surrounded by that many blind people. I kept my adventures to the bowling alley, restaurants, and bars to a handful to ensure I was well-rested and able to study. Learning to do everything in the dark required intense concentration, and I had already experienced missing out on a day because of dehydration after a night of fun. I had spent nine months in bed recovering from surgeries and cringed at the thought of losing any more time.

I arrived for the weekend at my Mission Street home, feeling energized and productive after my JAWS course at the LightHouse. My mom and sister had moved in and were helping me with the upkeep of my condo. It had been about ten years since I had lived with my family, and I was initially unsure it would work out. I told myself this was just another phase and that someday I would live on my own again, allowing myself to just enjoy the company. I was walking toward my bedroom when I felt something on the floor with my cane. I reached out and felt a clammy hand on the floor. I realized it was my mom's hand and yelled my sister's name. My sister's gasp filled the room, and I reminded myself that she was pregnant and that it was up to me to get our mom to the couch. My mom's mumbling told me that she was conscious and that most likely her sugar levels had dropped. I sprang toward the kitchen to get some orange juice and was stunned to hear my brother-in-law and sister freaking out. *Maybe because I can't see what is happening, I am able to handle the situation better,* I thought to myself. I dialed 911 as I handed my sister the cup of juice and instructed her to help mom sip. The paramedics arrived, and I explained my mom's medical history to them. I heard the men buckle and snap my mom as the strange voices left my apartment. I asked my brother-in-law to ride in the ambulance, since he was in better shape than my sister and me.

The next couple of hours were filled with that loud silence that follows chaos and tragedy. My cell rang and I was relieved to get positive news from the doctor. She said my mom had just suffered a diabetic attack and that she should be going home soon. "The paramedics were really impressed with you, Belo. They said you handled it better than people without any handicaps," added the doctor. I accepted the compliment, even though I did not think I did anything any of my blind friends like Lily or Tessa could not do. It then suddenly hit me: Maybe all blind people have an "S" on our chests that we simply can't see.

23

Handicap vs. Handicap

I had been at the OCB for exactly two months when I finally felt comfortable enough with my cane skills to venture out in San Francisco completely on my own. I started with short bus rides to places near my home and proceeded to elongate the routes until I finally tapped my way downtown. During my early trips on Muni, it truly surprised me how other disabled individuals and seniors would offer me their seats. I would hear plastic bags and tired limbs struggle to move as they made room for my young body to sit. On one occasion, an older woman in a walker slowly spoke to me in a smoky and agitated manner, "Take my spot; you are blind and shouldn't stand."

I realized I had conveniently landed on top of the handicap caste system and felt quite excited about the whole thing. It soon became second nature to hear crowds part in front of my white cane as I touched my way through Muni and BART.

One untraditionally warm San Francisco day, I decided to visit my old Inner Richmond district neighborhood. As usual, I quickly claimed a seat on the crowded 38 Geary bus. I was calmly listening to my iPod as the sun wrapped me in its warmth, when, suddenly, my moment of serenity came to a roaring end. I felt a heavy hand rapidly tapping my leg. I immediately pulled out my ear phones and said, "What's going on?"

A voice with extreme nasal qualities then responded, "Come on, kid; you are slowing all of us down. You are in my seat, so scoot."

I answered in a cocky tone, "I'm blind." I waved my VIP card in the form of a white stick.

The man shouted in an impatient voice, "Well, my chair stomps your stick, so move!"

The driver then echoed, "Son, you are sitting over the wheelchair attachments; you are going to have to move."

A woman bathed in Chanel No. 5 came to my aid and found another seat for me near the rear. Stunned, I remained quiet as I tried to understand how I could have been exiled from my promised and secure sanctuary. I heard the driver call my stop, and I made my way to the front of the bus. I then again heard that nasal voice say, "I am getting off here too, driver."

The bus had come to a complete stop by the time the man finished his sentence. I asked the driver, "Can I please step off first? I am in a rush and can't wait for you to unstrap the wheelchair."

I did not hear anything and assumed the driver nodded his head. I stepped off the bus, feeling relieved to get away from that nasal voice that sounded like a *Star Wars* character.

I took my time getting to the intersection and enjoyed the sun's pat on my back as I reacquainted myself with this familiar landscape. I was preparing to cross when I heard, "You are blocking the ramp, kid. Jeez, don't you know that is used for wheelchairs?!"

I quickly recognized that dungeon voice and replied, "I need it lined up to cross straight."

The man then said, "Can you see this, kid? It's my middle finger."

I proceeded to say, "Shouldn't you be in the bike lane?"

I began to cross the street and stopped at the curb to try to pick up any noise. I smiled when I did not hear him behind me. I took a few steps and then felt something wet hit me on my back. I quickly rubbed my hand on my T-shirt and sniffed my finger. I was shocked to find out it was tomato sauce and a few strands of noodles. I then felt more spaghetti hit my arm. For a quick moment, I thought about calling the police and then remembered how ineffective they had been for me in the past. I had a flashback in which I saw a small shopping center I used to frequent nearby and recalled a set of stairs descending off the humming street. I extended my cane and made an attempt to run. My cane found the stairs, and I rushed toward the bottom. I heard the man mumble something from the top of the stairwell, and I answered with a few laughs. I took a step back and realized that I was standing on a landing and had not reached the bottom. I tumbled and wrestled the brick steps behind me until I lay face down on the concrete. My skin then began to remember that rugged, surfaced stone floor where I was initiated into my world of darkness. I realized that the man in the chair also had a story and so did the other people who, for various reasons, must sit in the front of the bus. A nice man from the nearby pizzeria came to help me and brought me into the restaurant. He offered me a free soda, and I stayed and bought some lunch to go.

I decided not to take a cab and hopped back on the bus. I stood up the entire ride and let the older generations rest their aching bones. I smiled timidly as I declined seats and offers of help and made my way home where I enjoyed my humble slice of pizza.

24

Awake

I lay on my side, ignoring the sounds of voices and canes tapping that came from the hallway. I took a couple of deep breaths, desperately trying to relinquish my fears about the day and the summer season just being conceived. I heard Megean's, Nelson's, and Lily's voices coming from behind my door, and a few knocks shortly followed. I reluctantly dragged myself from the twin bed and opened the door. "Happy Birthday, Belo!" yelled a sea of excited voices.

Like in a game of Twister, I felt arms stretch and bend to wrap themselves around my body. Lily asked, "So, we're doin' the bowling alley tonight, right?"

Their joyful spirit coated me with energy and excitement, and my reluctance washed away. We made plans to head out around 5:00 PM, and I tasked Lily with the job of inviting everyone at school. They headed to the kitchenette down the hallway, and I promised to join them in a few minutes. As I dressed myself for class, I thought about my previous birthday when I had some vision and wished to get all of my sight back on the tiny flames that danced over the chocolate cake. I listened to my color identifier recite the different shades of denim that made up my pants collection, and I settled for the light gray with a white polo as I murmured,

"I should have just wished to keep what I had; I wouldn't need this thing." I waved the color-talking device in the air before tucking it into its pouch and heading out of my room for breakfast.

I saw shades of red and orange lights dance in my right eye and immediately sat up on my bed. Things no longer looked submerged in water, and there were traces of detail on my dresser and the pictures on the wall. I blinked a few times, feeling the tears rolling down my face. I had spent three weeks in total darkness and a week in a world where chairs waddled and people appeared like ghostly images in a horror film. I turned toward my nightstand and gasped when I was able to read the time on my alarm clock. I snagged my cell off the nearby table and dialed my friend Jeff. His phone only rang once, and I heard, "Happy Birthday, Belo!"

I smiled and walked to my mirrored closet doors and began to explore my face as I told Jeff about my magically restored vision. "Jeff, I can't believe it! Yesterday things still looked all foggy and shapeless, and now I can read the time a foot away from the clock."

Jeff said, "Belo, I told you it would come back. I have known you for ten years and know how strong and tough you can be."

I made plans to meet up with him later for a birthday lunch, threw the phone on the bed, and ran into the hallway. I knocked on my mom's door a few times and, unable to hold my excitement back, pushed her door open. I kneeled next to her head and whispered, "Mom, it's back; I can see again."

In a startled tone, she said, "Oh my god, it's a miracle."

We embraced each other and wiped each other's tears as I

tested my new vision in her room. "I can't make out what the letters say, but I can see a dark-skinned man on the screen," I said as I pointed at the TV.

My mom tightened her grip on my hand and said, "That's Barack Obama; he wants to be the president."

Although I had only been blind for a month, I knew the world hadn't stopped, and I had to catch up with it again. What I did not know then was that rather than feeling over-eager to regain my sighted life, I should have felt thankful for the lingering vision I did have.

I entered the OCB cafeteria and effortlessly picked up my food tray with my free hand and caned with the other toward the voices that gleefully chanted my name. I was met by another chorus of birthday wishes. I sat next to Amanda and began to answer the tumble of affectionate and inquisitive questions. "I'm twenty-eight. I'm a summer solstice baby. I make summer happen and plan to be at the bowling alley tonight," I said, as I sipped my coffee.

The warm weather deepened, forcing me to shed my spring ensemble for lighter summer gear. I felt the hot, dry air stroke my bare legs and arms while I walked to cooking class. It was almost strange to not feel sorrow when realizing that this was how all my birthdays would be moving forward—no more sun or blue skies and no concept of my aging face. I was finally awake.

25

Miss Magley

gingerly opened the door and walked toward the female voice at the far side of the room answering the phones. I proudly said, "I am here to see Christopher and Susan." The young voice asked me to take a seat, and I was relieved to recognize the furniture with the tip of my cane. It was the same stylish SOMA loft to which I had made numerous visits as an interviewee and client. I remembered the layout of the office. I saw a younger and more aggressive version of myself shaking hands with Susan Magley and Christopher, her right-hand man, five years prior. I had always wanted to work for Magley and Associates, yet I was always either off the job market or they weren't hiring. Our game of tag brought about a wonderful friendship between Team Magley and me. It was no surprise that they were among the first group of people to send flowers to my home and offer support in the days after the assault. Christopher and I kept in touch throughout my rehabilitation and discussed employment possibilities multiple times.

I was brought out of my haze by Christopher's charismatic baritone calling my name. I felt his hand shake mine and pat my shoulder twice and then heard another voice say, "Belo, it's Susan. You look great!" I grabbed onto her arm, and we all headed toward a conference room.

They both helped me to a chair, and we began to discuss the organization's needs and ways I could possibly help. I suppose it was because I knew them so well or maybe because I could not see the expressions on their faces, but I felt confident and able to succeed despite my blindness. I could hear them gasp with admiration when I demonstrated my Braille PDA and how JAWS worked on my laptop.

Beginning to stuff my tech toys back in my bag, I announced, "I'm also applying for a guide dog."

The small room erupted in clapping and cheering. Christopher bellowed, "Oh my goodness, we are so excited for you! What will you name the dog?"

I adjusted my tie and began to fill them in on the guide dog application process. "We don't get to name them, because they've done all their training under their given name. However, I am asking for a female and hoping for a real fierce name."

We all laughed for a few seconds before Susan added, "Well, Belo, I think this is going to work really well, and you'll be hearing back from us to talk money soon."

I unfolded my cane and started my journey back to the OCB. My cane tapped over broken cement and grooves in the sidewalk in a joyful tempo toward the bus stop. My usual frustration with the streets of downtown was no longer clouding my thoughts. I smiled every time someone bumped into me on the crowded 14 Mission line as I replayed the words of Miss Magley in my head that finally allowed me to imagine a future.

26

Blind Date

I was recording my homework assignment on my PDA when I heard Lily and Megean knock and yell my name from behind the door. I jumped to answer the banging, and my room quickly filled with laughing as both women tried to talk at the same time. I puckered my lips and whistled as loud as my lungs allowed. They both quieted down, and I began to ask questions. "Okay. So, what about this new guy?"

Lily's voice tumbled out as she described the new student. "Belo, he's in his late twenties and gay!"

I had met a few blind gay guys over the course of my rehabilitation the past year, but they were all middle-aged or older, their blindness often caused by HIV. Up until recently, I had put dating on hold and placed all my energy into completing the OCB curriculum. I never considered the possibility of hooking up with another student. I grabbed my cane, and we all headed out of my room to meet up with the new gay.

We three made our way to the TV room. While getting comfortable on the leather sofa, I asked Lily and Megean, "So, are you two sure he's gay?" They both insisted he was gay and that he sounded cute. "What does it mean to sound cute?"

"Duh, Belo, his voice is confident and friendly. Even though he is newly blind, he sounds pretty secure," Lily answered. We sang along to music videos while waiting for the new guy to show up.

I heard an unfamiliar and charismatic voice say, "Hi, I'm Kenny. I just started today." Lily helped him sit next to her. We all introduced ourselves, our cause of blindness, and the amount of sight we each possessed. Kenny told us he had lost his vision three months ago and had dropped out of an engineering program at Cal Poly. Like many of the other students, he had lost his sight from diabetes.

Lily jumped in, "That's what happened to me too, but at least you have some vision."

Kenny described how everything looked submerged in water. "It's hard to explain, kinda like looking through a fish bowl," he continued.

I felt my throat sting when I realized Kenny and I had the same medical procedure done. I knew perfectly well what Kenny was experiencing, since I went through the same thing before I lost my sight completely. I said, "It gets clearer with time. Then, one day, your eyes will be able to focus." I left out what had happened to me.

Megean disagreed, "I'm not sure about that, Belo. He could heal totally differently." Not wanting to argue, I suggested we grab dinner at the bowling alley. I noticed Kenny's tone go from social to fearful when he said, "I don't think I can get there. I'm not good with my cane."

I heard a cane snap and unfold, and Megean said, "Oh, don't worry. You can hold on to me." Although Kenny was not sitting near me, I could feel anxiety and panic come from his direction. We all made our way to the front of the school where we met up with Nelson. I heard kissing and giggling and assumed it was Lily and Nelson being affectionate.

Kenny got close to me and asked, "Are they together? I mean, they are both blind."

Megean and I both laughed, and I answered, "We're blind not dead!"

I was chosen to lead the group, and like ducklings marching toward a pond, we headed out to the bowling alley. Just like Tessa did, I pointed out obstacles for my friends tapping behind me. I could feel my gaydar go off every time Kenny said something. Although I had no idea what he looked like, I began to feel drawn to him.

Kenny chuckled and said, "This is crazy, the blind leading the blind."

I sighed and retorted, "Most old sayings about the blind are not true, but you will find that out on your own."

We entered Albany Bowl and were seated by our usual friendly waitress. I felt her petite, soft hand tuck a strand of hair behind my ear and whisper, "Belo, I'll sit the new guy next to you."

I began to feel confused by the urge to flirt with Kenny, because I was unsure how to do so. Although I had dated and even had a boyfriend by now, I had relied on their ability to see and let them take the role of the driver in the courtship.

Over our burgers and fries, we all took turns filling Kenny in on the OCB curriculum and staff. Lily said, "Most importantly, take your time learning and expect to have a few bad days here and there."

I began to analyze my insecurity and figured that if I could get Kenny to confirm he was gay, it would make me more comfortable flirting with him. I was still trying to form the question in my head when Kenny asked, "So, Belo, are you single?"

I sensed my face get warm and took a sip of water before

answering, "My boyfriend and I broke up two months ago. What about you?"

He began to tell the group about his last relationship with a guy from Sacramento, which had recently ended. I felt Lily squeeze my hand and heard her tell Kenny that the rest of them were leaving but that I could help him get back to school.

When Kenny and I were alone, we quickly began to ask each other questions. I suggested we grab a drink at the bar next door, and Kenny calmly accepted. I offered him my hand, and I felt him tense up. He reminded me we were at a straight establishment and that holding my hand would not be a good move. I smiled and responded, "People will see our white sticks and see two blind guys helping each other." He did not say anything, and in a matter of seconds, I felt his fingers trail my arm and clasp my hand. I led the way to the bar next door, and with my cane, I found two empty seats.

Kenny gasped before asking, "How did you find the chairs? That is fuckin' awesome!" I felt giddy and explained how having mobility lessons every day at OCB helped me build strong cane skills.

I added, "I want a guide dog and have been putting in extra hours to prepare for the exam next month."

We ordered a drink and filled each other in on our experiences in the gay world. We were both equally annoyed with the novelty treatment or being handled like fragile objects. The bar was playing music from the '90s, and we began to reminisce. Our laughter filled the lonely dive, as I enjoyed my first blind date.

27

Sunshine

I kept waking up every two hours, only to find out it was too early to get up. Although I needed as much rest as possible to prepare for the big day ahead, I still could not find sleep deeply until the scent of morning was creeping into the air. It must have been the tenth time I hit my talking alarm clock, when I finally heard the female *Mission Impossible* voice say, "Good morning; it's 7:00 AM."

I rose and began to get ready for a shower. I turned the radio on and caught a quick sound bite of the weather forecast for the day. "It will be a hot, hot, hot day," announced the female radio personality. I got in the shower and began to think about my graduation from OCB only a few hours away. The warm mist and the soap's lather coated me. I thought about the job offer at Magley & Associates I had accepted and the fact that I would no longer be surrounded by blind people once I exited the school's grounds. I turned the water faucet off and wrapped myself in a clean towel. I was back in my room when I heard the same DJ say, "Today is definitely a bikini day!"

I reached for my clothes as a male voice added, "Let me play this song for you then." I was fully dressed when I was distracted by the very familiar tune. "You are my sunshine, my only sunshine; you make me happy when skies are gray ..."

I grew up hearing these lyrics in movies and commercials. Nevertheless, those words never meant anything to me until that morning. "So, please don't take my sunshine away."

The moment I heard these words, I felt my chest cave in. I suddenly realized that although I had completed the nine-month OCB curriculum in a third of the time and was a success story at the LightHouse, it had not diminished the fact that my sunshine had been taken away. The female announcer said, "It's only 7:30 a.m., and I already need my shades."

My breathing had become shallow, and I staggered toward the window. I could feel the sun's rays as I lay my hand flat on the glass. It was suddenly suffocating to feel the light on my fingertips but not be able to see it. I climbed on top of my desk, knocking a few items to the floor. I pressed my face and as much of my body as possible to the tepid glass, attempting to absorb as much as the sun would let me. I felt the tears glide between the glass and my cheek. My hands began to shake, and other muscles followed them. The air thickened, and it became a struggle to breathe. I gasped, "God, please help me."

I was shocked to hear his name roll off my tongue. In the past eighteen months, I never blamed God for any of my mishaps, because I felt that the only people to blame were my attackers. However, I also had not called on him. In that moment, for the first time, I asked for his help and compassion as the room tried to squeeze the air out of my lungs.

The ringing of the phone cut into my moment of panic. Still panting, I let out a pathetic "Hello?"

My friend Tessa's bubbly "Hi, baby" calmed my breathing and slowed the pounding in head.

Her cheeriness soothed me, and I was almost normal when I heard my classmates bang on the door, "Hey, Belo. Let's go to breakfast."

Lily, Nelson, and Megean followed me to the cafeteria. The sun's rays caressed my face and body throughout the day as I said my goodbyes to my classmates and teachers. Its warm touch made me feel alive but also reminded me of the world that had been taken from me. Although I was not an angel, I knew I was not a bad person. A clear conscience gave me hope in the world I could no longer see. I would never see the sun rise or set again, but I still had my connection to it.

28

Team Magley

The IT manager and I started to unpack boxes in my cubicle. I was fortunate enough to have gotten a few job offers, but I decided to accept the offer from Magley and Associates because I wanted to have a successful transition back to the workforce. Most of the team I would be working with had all met me at some point during my staffing career, which was very comforting to me. The staffing industry is highly competitive, and I was unsure of how supportive and patient a group of strangers would be.

The IT manager seemed quite impressed with all the gadgets the Department of Rehabilitation bought for me. Every other sentence included a "cool" or "nifty" as we set up my station. My rehab counselor, Jacob, was a key player in helping me go from a bitter young man without any mobility and hope to a positive, independent traveler, who—a year after the assault—was working and well-versed in adaptive technology. Jacob, unlike some of the counselors my blind friends had, was responsive and kept me motivated while at the LightHouse and at OCB.

Christopher walked to my desk and told me the morning staff meeting would be starting in five minutes. To my surprise, I did not feel anxious or nervous but deeply happy.

I cued up my PDA and headed down the hallway for my first work meeting.

I was greeted by the smell of freshly made coffee and bagels and was helped to a seat by one of my new coworkers. Although bagels and coffee are part of my morning ritual, I was too self-conscious of making a mess and decided to stick to a bottle of orange juice. Also, I was unsure if I could manage typing Braille on my PDA, listening to my computer with my earpiece, paying attention to the people speaking, and eating all at the same time.

Someday, I might be capable of doing everything my sighted coworkers did, but I would have to build to it. The meeting started off with my introduction to the agency and segued into a discussion of key accounts. I was slightly surprised that I was still familiar with staffing best practices and technology, since the industry seemed to change so quickly. I was relieved to find that I could still contribute to the collective. At the end of the powwow, I was assigned to manage a major account.

I headed back to my desk and started to introduce myself via phone and email to our various customers. Part of me wanted to tell them I was blind and new at juggling hearing JAWS with my left ear, typing on a keyboard, and using the phone with my right ear. My brain felt like putty being pulled in so many directions, and I constantly asked people to repeat themselves. Instead, I resorted to humor with cheesy lines, like, "I'm barely on my first cup of coffee," and "I think my brain still thinks it's Saturday," to buy me time to navigate by sound to the proper screens and fields. After an hour, my temples began to ring. I was interrupted by Christopher asking me to join him for lunch.

The lunch was brief, and it seemed almost immediate that we headed back to the office. I was surprised to find a few

email and phone messages from former colleagues responding to my updated information on the networking sites. They
all wondered where I had disappeared to and wanted to
know what was new with me. I figured telling them I'd been
in rehab for the last year would be confusing and misleading.
I scheduled a few catch-up lunches for the following weeks. I
was unsure how I would present my blind side to old friends.

I continued to get acquainted with the company's
systems and policies and peppered in a few phone inter-
views throughout the day. In the late afternoon, I decided to
take a quick break on the roof deck to help clear my ringing
ears. I was enjoying the cool, crisp air, when I was startled
by a man's voice asking, "Are you related to Belo Cipriani?"
Turning toward the voice, I nodded but did not say anything.
I suppose my post-traumatic stress disorder can sometimes
make me skittish. The guy continued, "You guys are identi-
cal! If it wasn't for the white cane, you guys could pass for
twins. Well, tell him Dan says hello."

I could not recognize the voice but figured I had made
some type of impact on this guy's life for him to approach a
so-called stranger. Tapping my cane back to the office, I made
the decision not to tell anyone I was blind unless I really had
to. After all, my role would allow me to perform most trans-
actions over the phone, and I did not want to be known as the
blind recruiter.

I arrived at my cubical and heard chatter and glasses
clinking. "There you are, Belo!" A group of voices said,
"Welcome to Team Magley!" I was handed a glass of wine.
Everyone congratulated me on my first day, clicking my glass
while making their rounds. I smiled and decided to push all
my concerns to the following day.

29

The Force

A cheerful man greeted us and showed Fernando and me to our table on the back patio. Nirvana in the Castro District was one of those rare places I could still enjoy without sight. As I began to revisit venues I frequented during my vision era, I discovered that most of them were too loud and crowded, making them tough to navigate with my cane. The waterfall that echoed all around me and the fresh-flower scent that lingered encouraged my muscles to relax. I was listening to Fernando read the menu when I accidentally knocked my silverware to the floor. I felt a vibration on my arm and quickly snagged the spoon off the paved stones. I smiled and rubbed sanitizer on my hands as I said, "I wasn't planning on using my spoon anyway; they have good spring rolls here."

Fernando chuckled and asked with his sexy Cuban accent, "How did you know where the spoon was? It was like you could see it."

I paused and pointed my face toward the direction of his voice, saying, "I used the Force." His laughter moved into snorting and coughing territory.

I hoped my distaste for his nerdy laugh did not show too badly, as I heard him sip his water and say, "That is what I like about you the most, your humor."

The next day, I practiced throwing various objects on different floor surfaces. I dropped coins on the wooden boards of my apartment and then switched to throwing my shoe a few feet in front of me on the carpet. I noticed a range in the vibration that bounced off my skin. It was almost as if my pores could hear. I began to feel like a mutant coming into his powers. I thought about the blind guy on *Oprah*, who moved around caneless. Like a handful of blind people I know, he relied on echo location to get around. I never developed the echo location skill and felt deeply mediocre relying solely on my cane.

I picked up the things I had been throwing on the floor and started to get ready for my date. Although I completed my rehabilitation and was hired by a noted and reputable consulting firm, I had still been insecure about the pudginess left from my tedious recovery. I did not begin to feel confident until I was able to fit into the clothes I purchased with sight. I smiled as I blow-dried my hair and thought about my date with Sascha. I thought about ways I could use my new sensory trick to impress him. Perhaps, this vibration I sensed on my skin was what was going to help me find a "man friend." I was unsure why or how the skin vibration worked, but I was excited about the possibilities.

I called for a cab and knocked at my sister's room before leaving my condo. I told her and my brother in-law that I would be at The Café in the Castro District and that I would call at 1 a.m. to check in. I still felt awkward relying on my baby sister as a backup plan, but I knew it was the smart thing to do. My sister asked, "Are you going out with Fernando?"

I shyly shook my head and said, "No, um, I am hanging out with this Russian guy I met last week."

She patted my shoulder and told me to be careful. The

intercom began to ring, and I made my way to Mission Street and boarded the cab.

A few moments later, I texted Sascha to let him know I had arrived at the bar and waited on the curb for him to come meet me. I heard a car park two feet away, and a few women laughed as they slammed the doors. I heard something hit the cement, and I felt that vibration again on my right arm. I shouted, "I think you dropped something!"

I heard a girl say, "Oh my God, I dropped my keys. You are like Daredevil or something." I smiled, and I felt the girl's minty breath on my face and heard her say, "If you show up at The Café, I will buy ya a drink."

I nodded and told her I would be there shortly. I checked my watch and noticed only five minutes had gone by, but it felt more like an hour. I thought back to our first chat in which I confessed my blindness and how surprised I was that he seemed unaffected by the news. I was growing sick with worry that Sascha had changed his mind about dating a blind guy, when I heard, "Belo, it's Sascha; give me a hug."

His embrace was warm, and it was mesmerizing to connect with another person on an intimate level. It was my first time meeting him, and, by his embrace, I could tell he was totally my type—fit and taller than I, with pierced ears. He pulled me by my hand and paid my cover at the entrance. We climbed a few stairs, reached a small round table, and took a seat. The music was making the floor vibrate, and I struggled to make out what Sascha was saying. His accent went from sexy to cryptic in seconds, leaving me with no other option than to smile politely. I ordered a beer and rejected Sascha's suggestion to take a shot with him. I told him, "I can't get too crazy; I have to make it home." He squeezed my hand and went to get our drinks.

I sensed the club fill with gyrating bodies, and I felt my

stomach knot as I realized ten minutes had passed and there was no sign of Sascha anywhere. I then conjured images of his meeting a cute guy at the bar and forgetting all about me. After all, I had committed a similar crime plenty of times myself when I had vision. I had just leaped off the bar stool to leave the club, when I felt someone cup my arm and place a cold glass bottle in my hand. I took a swig without hesitation and almost spit the sweet Belgium beer out of my mouth. I shouted toward Sascha, "I don't like sweet beers."

I then heard, "What did you say?"

I reached into the air and found his shoulder. I pulled his body toward mine to speak into his ear and was met by a pair of moist cold lips that slowly trailed up my neck toward my lips before teasing my tongue. I pulled my cane out of my jacket and suggested we move out to one of the patios when I felt the same cold lips on my ear ask, "What is that stick for?"

I suddenly remembered how dark and misleading clubs are, and I began to feel like someone who had their drink spiked at a college party when I heard another voice behind me say, "Belo, what the hell is this?"

I realized it had to be Sascha even though I could not really recognize his voice over the loud hip-hop song. I shouted toward the new voice, "I thought it was you!"

I felt Sascha lean into me and heard the disappointment in his voice, as he said, "How could you not tell the difference? We are wearing different clothing, and I'm taller. I'm sure we even smell different."

I stood there quietly trying to come up with good answers for his questions. I could now smell Sascha's spicy cologne, which did not at all resemble the citrus fragrance of the mysterious kisser. Sascha angrily wished me a good night, and I sat back on my chair. I felt abandoned, despite the possibility that Sascha could have just moved to a nearby table. John

"Kiss" Doe had also vanished, and, bitterly, I decided to leave the club.

A bus boy helped me flag down a cab, and I headed back home feeling confused and annoyed by my blindness. I realized that no matter how many new superhero tricks I developed, I would never have my sight back. Smell, hearing, and touch would never substitute completely for the ability to see things and make accurate decisions. My other senses would get stronger with time, but I would always be guessing to some degree. Maybe someday I would be able to trust the forces that help me, but until then, I should take more time getting to know who I have become.

30

Hi, Dad

Before I had a dog of my own, I found it absurd and often laughed at people who referred to their dogs as kids. I recall a particular sun-filled Saturday, while enjoying a day of relaxation in Chaska, Minnesota. My sister interrupted our conversation to call her dog Chloe at the kennel. I nearly spit out my lovely glass of pinot, when I heard the words, "Hello, this is Chloe's mom, checking on her ..."

Unlike my sister, I was blinded by my vision of doggy drool on my clothes and the sneaky dog hair that makes its way to every part of one's wardrobe. I could not believe any dog would be worth all that work and time.

As I progressed in my rehabilitation, I began to hear all sorts of compelling stories about different guide dog teams and the adventures they went on; however, with my newly heightened sense of smell, the guide dog idea seemed not only too much work, but extremely full of stench.

One wet afternoon, I attempted to cross the extremely unfriendly intersection of Mission and Geneva. The rain was distorting my hearing, and I felt like I was standing in the eye of the storm. Suddenly, I heard jingles coming in my direction. I was not familiar with this type of sound and thought the rain was amplifying some distant noise. I felt the jingles stop right next to me, and I figured out it was the harness of a guide dog that was making its way to the curb of the busy street. A powerful and confident voice said, "Sally, forward!" Then, the jingles faded into the sea of horns and crackling power lines on which the buses float.

I continued to try to read my line of traffic to cross, and my frustration was quickly taking over when a soft, dry voice said, "Can I help you cross the street?"

The ancient voice sounded like he had waited eons to murmur those words. Embarrassed and full of shame, I remained silent and stretched my hand out. I found a thin arm wrapped in wet, hard plastic, which I tried very hard not to clutch. After crossing what seemed to me like the intersection that connected North America to Africa, we finally reached our finish line in the shape of a curb. Then the man said, "You should get a dog." I nodded and began to make my way home. It always surprises me how strangers often give the best advice and how they come to it with speed and ease.

One cold and damp February afternoon, a few months later, Gina O'Conner from Guide Dogs for the Blind came into my dorm room, bringing with her a female yellow lab who she announced as Madge. I could feel the dog's excitement and heard that familiar jingle coming from her collar. Gina then handed the leash over to me, and Madge launched at full speed. Her warm tongue and head rubbing against my leg said, "Hi, Dad!"

31

Belo and Yellow

We had been instructed to spend the next hour playing with our dogs and to keep the doors to our rooms open. I heard Kim and her roommates' voices from across the hallway, and I moved closer to the door as I called, "So, who did you get paired up with?"

Kim answered, "Oh, um, I have Melody; she's a yellow lab."

Her roommate quickly interjected, "I have Mica, and he's a red lab."

I heard my phone ring and excused myself as I pulled Madge's leash and clumsily reached for my phone on the bed.

Tessa and I had been playing phone tag ever since I arrived at Guide Dogs for the Blind. The rigorous training schedule started immediately after my arrival on the San Rafael campus, and there was a whirlwind of information and emotions bunched into my first three days. I answered with, "It's a girl!"

"Oh my gosh. That is so awesome! The best part is that you don't gotta worry about stretch marks," she replied.

We both giggled, and I began to tell her about walking with a stuffed dog on wheels named Juno the first two days.

"It was funny; we had to talk to and correct Juno. I felt like a little girl at a tea party," I told her.

"I'm sure you were really good at that!" Tessa hissed.

"Forget you, dumb-ass!" I responded with a hardy laugh.

I continued to go over the third day when we got to work with guide dogs in training. I described how it felt like I was flying when I walked with those first dogs. Although they varied drastically in size, the speed and thrill was immensely intoxicating. "Traveling with a cane is like trying to get around on a tricycle, while walking with a guide dog is like riding a motorcycle," I added.

I told Tessa I had just met Madge half an hour before her call. I was eager to take her out on a spin but was told we would not get to do any guide work until the following day. The first day was all about bonding with our new mates. On this note, Tessa and I said our goodbyes.

I took a deep breath and collapsed on the tiled floor. I smiled as I reflected on all the hours of mobility training at the LightHouse and OCB I had endured to arrive at this phase of my sightless life. The trailing of buildings, getting lost in people's driveways, and constantly stabbing myself with the cane were all a thing of the past now. My moment of reflection was interrupted by an outrageously wet tongue on my cheek. "Oh, oh, oh, wait no, stop, heel." My words morphed into laughter as Madge attacked my face.

I heard a woman scream, "Oh my gosh; my dog is gone! Help! My dog is gone!" I jumped up and grabbed my cane, which hung near the door.

I was about to step out and remembered Madge. "Oh, um, come." Her leash slid across the hard floor, and I smiled when I felt her head rub my left knee. Reaching out for the leather rope, I began to make my way down the hall. I struggled to walk straight as Madge kept trying to lead. I said,

"No, heel," yet she continued to want to walk the other direction. I gave Madge her first correction, and she let me lead for about five seconds and then began to jump around, tangling my legs with her leash.

I heard Amanda ask, "Belo, is that you?"

I mumbled, "Yeah, it's me."

Amanda and I had attended OCB and had gone through the guide dog application process together. Although my other classmates seemed nice and professional, it was extremely comforting to have a friend in the program. "Oh, Belo, Ms. Yvette's dog is missing. My poor roomie is devastated."

She took a step and placed her hand on my shoulder. We both began to chuckle, and I asked, "How? We just got them."

I heard one of the instructors at a distance trying to get Ms. Yvette to calm down as a second instructor called everyone to the seminar room.

My classmates were from various corners of the country and ranged in age from twentysomethings to retired people. As I got to know each one better, I became more impressed and proud of being grouped with such successful blind men and women. Everyone had a career or held significant volunteer roles with nonprofit organizations. They were a steep contrast to my former peers at OCB, because they no longer struggled with day-to-day tasks like cleaning or cooking. They had conquered blindness and were more preoccupied with universal concerns like buying a home or sending a child to college. My cohorts consisted of people receiving their first guide dog, yet it was obvious that I had the least experience with canines. All of the other guides sat silent and undetected to my ears, while Madge kept interrupting the class. My embarrassment grew into frustration as the voices around me asked me to please control my dog. The instructor adjourned the class, and the teams quietly made their way to dinner.

Despite all the people and dogs present in the dining hall, the noise level remained low. I was the last person to reach my table after Madge insisted on greeting all her kennel mates along the way. I finally reached my seat and heard everyone at the table laughing. Kim said, "Did you guys hear that Ms. Yvette had accidentally placed her dog in one of the empty bedrooms, which is why she couldn't find him?"

I knew Ms. Yvette's missing dog story was hilarious, but I could not concentrate on anything but Madge sniffing the other dogs and trying to wander to the other tables. Kim added, "I don't know why they paired you with such a hyper dog; you are so mellow."

I answered, "She is just getting used to me," secretly wishing my words were true.

I was bringing my spoon to my lips when Madge sprung toward Kim's dog. I heard the spoon rattle on the hard floor and quickly began to wipe the vegetables and rice off my shirt. I never imagined the guide dog lifestyle would be so challenging and began to feel like a teen parent. I pulled the leash toward me and cried, "Madge, please listen to me!"

Silence took over the room as I heard the clinking of silverware come to a sudden stop and a pair of shoes run in my direction. "Belo, what's wrong?" inquired one of the female instructors gently.

In a defeated tone, I replied, "She's not listening to me."

She patted my shoulder and told me that all dogs test their owners at some point and that Madge was doing it right at the beginning. The chatter in the hall resumed as the instructor continued to explain ways I could be more assertive.

I was contemplating packing my bags that moment

and heading back to San Francisco, when I felt Madge lick my fingertips. I shifted my thoughts to Madge's journey to becoming a guide dog: the year she spent learning basic social skills with her puppy raisers and the months it took to complete the guide dog training. Her life had been full of major changes, culminating in the arrival of some short guy with big hair who probably wore too much cologne. I told Madge it would be okay and that I had her back. She curled her body around my leg and rested her head on my foot. The teacher patted me again as she walked away.

32

Traffic

"Belo, wake up. Class is starting," Amanda whispered. I cleared my throat and realized I had dozed off on the ridiculously soft couch. I panicked for a second and trailed my leash until I found Madge stretched out on the carpet. I sighed and shifted my tired body toward Amanda. "I don't know if I can do it, Belo. My knee be all swollen," continued Amanda in her Cajun accent.

I softly answered, "You're going to be fine. We'll both graduate in a week and laugh at ourselves for sounding like a pair of weaklings."

Madge and I had been training for the last three weeks, and I was just getting used to traveling with a guide dog. It felt surreal to move with such intense velocity and feel graceful at the same time. I no longer had the connection to my environment that I had with my cane, forcing me to learn to pick up new cues through sound and scent. I now paid attention to people shuffling out of doors to identify entrances and used smells from restaurants or coffee shops to mark locations. My instructors constantly reminded me to trust my dog, since I sometimes got into trouble for overriding Madge's guide work. I noticed some of my other classmates had already bonded with their guides, which made their outings a total breeze. I remained anxious as Madge and I would struggle from time to time through the various routes and obstacles. I knew I was more than halfway through the program and put all my energy into making our partnership a successful one.

Amanda and I quieted down when we heard the instructor go over the day's agenda. "Okay, so today is quite busy," the instructor added.

I smiled and pinched Amanda's arm as I said, "Every day is quite busy here."

Each day started at 5:30 AM and continued with a few breaks until 8:30 PM. The guide dog training was by far the most challenging thing I had experienced in my life, more challenging than my martial arts training and college combined. It constantly tested both my spirit and bones in ways that felt foreign to me. The instructor continued with, "We will also be doing a traffic obstacle course with you guys today."

Madge and I had struggled from time to time with some of the previous courses, and I grew worried as the details of the traffic scenario were revealed to us. The class continued with a lecture on vet care that segued into an obedience lesson. However, as the day proceeded, I became more nervous about the traffic course.

After a short bus ride to the downtown campus, Amanda and I waited our turn in one of the small rooms. Amanda asked, "So, how are you feelin' about the traffic test?"

Wanting to keep my composure, I avoided her question and replied, "It's pouring outside; I hope it stops by the time they get to me."

Amanda dropped the issue and began to talk about her family. I felt my knees tremble when a cheery voice called my name. Madge shook a few times before guiding me outside the building. The teacher went over the route and mentioned there would be staff members along the way in case I ran into trouble. The rain intensified as Madge and I took on the wet pavement. I gave Madge directions, and she executed them all with ease, despite her soaked coat and harness. I could not trust my hearing as the rain had changed the way everything sounded, making me place more trust in Madge. We were almost to the finish line, and I could feel a wiggle-wiggle through the handle on the harness that told me she was alert and watching out for me. It was the deepest connection I had felt with Madge. Our guide work began to feel like a dance as our movements became synchronized. I was feeling like a seagull coasting along the shoreline when Madge came to a sudden halt. She crossed her body in front of me, blocking my path completely. She had never done anything like this before, and I decided to let go and listen to her. I heard the instructor on my right say, "You guys did great; you are at a driveway and a hybrid just pulled in." I feared hybrids, because they made no sound. I leaned down and gave Madge a big hug. I could not see the rain but could feel it on Madge and on my face as we embraced each other. After that moment, I was no longer afraid.

33

Interdependence Day

Most of my deepest memories involve an animal companion of some kind—some more traditional like my Siamese cats Ryu and Mishee and others more uncommon like my pet chicken Monica. Whatever current phase or fad I was experiencing growing up, I always found myself seeking the company of my nonhuman friends.

Although I firmly believe that all animals are able to provide affection and support of some kind, I never expected any of my pets to solve my problems. I was in complete darkness about the ability to be interdependent with a dog and trust her with my life on a daily basis. Some dogs can roll over or play catch; I had discovered that mine could find me a seat on the bus and help me cross the busiest of streets. Madge and I had become a fierce team, able to face any type of barricade. Our connection hovered around telepathic as we could bend and stretch our bodies to complement each other's movement. Our guide work had become seamless, allowing me to bask in the joy of this unique partnership very few get to experience.

During a lesson, Amanda fell and was sent home to finish the program through private instruction. This event pushed me to socialize with the other students and allowed me to make new connections. Melody, Kim's guide dog, and Madge are litter mates, and they would seek each other out to play. It was through this sisterhood that I learned Kim was a lesbian. It felt deeply therapeutic to share concerns and stories with someone who understood what it felt like to be a multiple minority.

On a cold and quiet evening, Kim and I and a couple of other of students went out for a drink. It was over a chocolate martini that Kim brought something I had not thought of to my attention. "So, Belo, do you think it will be easier to date now that we have dogs?"

I could feel the creases around my mouth and eyes turn down in worry as Kim's words reached me. During the three-month guide dog application process, it had never occurred to me how a guide dog would impact my romantic relationships. Among my classmates, I was the newest member to blindhood. I had been so focused on surviving in the sightless world that every time I was reminded of common social concerns, they would hit me like a cold gust of wind. Attempting to sound positive, I replied, "Oh, I'm sure it will be fun and exciting." I then asked Kim, "If you could get your sight back through some medical procedure, would you go for it?"

"Absolutely not! I am who I am because I'm blind, and if I had sight, I would be someone else. I like myself," she responded in a firm tone. Kim's words echoed in my head as the creamy vodka drink seduced my tongue.

Back at my dorm, Madge and I played a quick game of tug-of-war before I wrapped her in one of my sweaters and called it a night. In bed, I wrestled my sheets as I struggled to sleep through Madge's snoring. I was slowly falling back into some of my sighted habits as I gained mastery of blind technology. Just like I did in my teens and right before the assault, I sought comfort in cyberspace. I never thought I would one day surf the net with my body flat on the bed and hitting only one or two keys. Adaptive technology had removed watery eyes and a sore neck and back. My screen-less Braille PDA was simplistic in its square design and rows of round buttons, yet it was my pass into the online world. I could listen to the spoken menus in any position, allowing me to truly become one with my miniature computer.

I logged on to a popular gay chat room that my friend LeShawn had told me about. He had also been nice enough to post a picture of me on the site. I feared the day someone would notice my blindness through my snapshot and always paused for a few minutes before entering any chat room.

I began to chat with a guy named Alex who seemed like the lead in a Spanish novella. He worked for a law firm in Palo Alto, but had recently bought a trendy condo in San Francisco's hip North Beach district. It was getting late, and I remembered I was to meet Madge's puppy raisers before the graduation ceremony the next day. I had already typed my goodbye message, when Alex asked if he could call me to say good night. When I had vision, I would have considered that line corny and would have walked away. I now found it sweet and exciting. The good-night call turned into an hour of jokes and storytelling. His radio announcer voice made me feel giddy every time he asked me anything. I heard Madge shake a couple of times before placing her paw on my leg. I asked the most important question of the evening, "Alex, do you like dogs?"

He chuckled before answering, "Um, it's okay if you have one. I hope you are not one of those crazy people who bring their dogs everywhere."

I wondered if Alex would have been that honest if he

knew I was blind and had a guide dog. For safety reasons, I made it a habit not to tell people about my disability until I felt completely comfortable, which often took more than one phone conversation. With the exception of Paul who confessed his deafness to me in a chat room, I had always waited to hear their voices to determine whether or not to reveal my blind side. I remained quiet and leaned down to rub Madge's ear. Alex continued, saying, "I hope you understand I have a brand-new BMW. Not really crazy about pets, but again you are free to have whatever makes you happy." Aggravated, I wished him a good night and turned my cell phone off. I gave Madge a hug and went to bed.

The next morning, I began to pack and straighten out what had been my home for the last few weeks. Still annoyed by Alex's comments, I sat on the floor next to Madge and began to tell her about my run-in with the man without a soul. I said, "There is something wrong with people who don't like animals." Madge licked my hand, and I smiled as I admired her ability to go from serious to funny.

Madge and I made our way to the meet-and-greet room to wait for her puppy raisers. I did not know much about them other than they were coming from L.A. to see us graduate. The noise level increased as I heard my classmates meet their puppy raisers. I was petting Madge when I heard, "There's our little girl. Don, look, she is all grown up!"

After a few introductions and handshakes, I handed the leash over to Don and Nancy. I could feel Madge's tail burst with excitement as it tapped my leg a few times. Nancy and Don were warm and attentive. We found some chairs and began to get to know each other. I told them how much I loved Madge and how thankful I was to them for raising her the first year of her life. I learned that Madge was the first puppy they raised and seeing her become such a mature and hardworking guide inspired them to keep raising more puppies. Nancy said, "She was waiting for you, Belo. It was her destiny to become your guide." Nancy's words made me feel whole as I realized I had just gained a soul mate.

34

Dirty Laundry

was walking in downtown San Francisco, desperately looking for Madge. The streets were filled with people zipping through piles of foam that were causing a glare, making it hard to focus any of the faces walking by. I picked up a faint whimper and began to dig through the foam. I saw my hands and the foam fade into complete darkness, and I realized I was dreaming. I heard Madge whimper a second time, and I quickly kicked my sheets off and made my way to her crate. I unhinged the metal door and smiled when I felt her warm body wrapped in her blanket and realized she was also dreaming. Madge sprang up and, with gusto, shook a few times before kissing me on my cheek. I began to chuckle and asked, "Are you nervous too?" Madge and I had just completed the four-week training at Guide Dogs for the Blind in San Rafael and now were ready to return to work at Magley & Associates. I slowly slid my fingers over Madge's velvety ears and reflected on the past month of strenuous course work through airport corridors, late-night walks in San Rafael, and the early relieving schedule that had often been accompanied by the cold February rain. It was very comforting to know that I would no longer have to face the world alone. I now had a partner that loved me unconditionally, something I had never experienced in all my years of sight.

My moment of reflection was interrupted by my new chaotic alarm clock that sounded like bells and whistles from a '50s game show. I closed Madge's crate and thumb-wrestled a set of round buttons, anxiously trying to eliminate the noise. I ended up pulling out the batteries, since I had forgotten how to use my clock. I suppose that is what happens when one leaves for a month. I thought to myself, "Crap, this is not how I wanted to start out this day." I grabbed my cell and checked the time. "It's 6:45 a.m.," said the male phonics voice.

I immediately hopped in the shower and began to get ready. I repeated aloud all the different guide dog commands that I was afraid I might forget during a time of crisis. I used the training name of Juno because I did not want to confuse Madge, just in case she was listening. I said, "Juno, hop up," as I squeezed shampoo on my hand, and "Juno, halt," as I dried my arms and threw some clothes on. This went on for a few minutes while I continued to prepare for our big San Francisco debut. I got Madge out of her crate and took her out to my patio for relieving, and then I fed her and prepared her snack bag. I harnessed her up and put her on a down command in my room. I headed back to the kitchen where I jammed her snack pouch in a duffel bag that also carried her toys, extra leash, blanket, and bowls. Smiling, I whispered, "This feels like a diaper bag."

I said, "Madge, come." I heard the jingles on her collar make their way toward me. I grabbed the handle on her harness and said with excitement, "Madge, let's go." We exited my condo and made our way down the stairs that led to Mission Street. I opened the door and was saluted by chaos outside. I paused for a few seconds, since it felt unnatural to leave my home without my cane. I cleared my throat and said, "Madge, bus stop." We took a few steps, and I felt the crowd of people all waiting for the express bus.

I heard a pair of high heels tap the cement and make their way toward me. A young woman said, "I am so glad you got a dog."

Unsure of how to respond, I answered, "Thanks!"

I felt, more than heard, the power lines popping above me and knew the bus was approaching. This familiar sound used to make me nervous, since this would be the time where I would have to depend on some kind soul to help me find the entrance to the bus. Now, I remained in total ease, knowing Madge could find the door with no problem. The bus came to a stop, and I said, "Madge, inside," and she effortlessly took me toward the steps.

The driver greeted me, saying, "What a beautiful dog! I am glad you finally got one." I showed him my teeth, attempting to smile, as I flashed my pass.

I remained quiet, trying desperately to think of something witty to use as a reply. I remembered there was a group of people behind me, and I gave up and realized Madge had taken me toward a seat. Madge placed herself next to me, and the bus began to move. I could feel the gazes of everyone around me. I heard all sorts of dialects and languages bounce off the windows. The only one I understood was *"perro, perro!"* I figured out they were pointing at Madge, but I knew it was not malicious, and I just smiled toward the back of the bus.

The twenty-minute bus ride was a delight; it seemed like everyone on the bus complimented Madge somehow. It felt so good to be treated and addressed like a sighted person. No one sped timidly past me, and no one asked how much I could see or if I had been born blind. Madge got all the attention, and I was perfectly fine with that arrangement. It became obvious to me that in the last few months I had become a part of the daily lives of many of these unfamiliar voices. The driver announced my stop, and I got ready to step off the Muni. I heard a couple of voices say, "Bye, doggie!" behind me, and I began to make my way toward Second and Howard.

Infused with confidence, I strolled down the streets of downtown like a celebrity making his way to a podium to collect an award. I felt Madge crab-walking, and I knew she was letting me know we were passing our office building. I calmly said, "Madge, door," and she pulled me toward the glass door.

I entered the lobby where a man shouted, "What a great-looking dog."

"Thank you," I replied.

The man then said with some hesitation, "Um, I don't mean to get into your business, but I think you should check your dog's mouth." I reached over and felt a garment in her mouth. I gently pulled it away and realized it was a pair of my boxers.

35

Glow Stick

I could smell the musky cologne on him before he took a few steps and hugged me. "Hey, sexy! No Madge today?" he cried as I felt his thin body under a wool sweater.

"Duh, Nate. She's not twenty-one," I answered playfully. Grabbing his arm, we laughed and strolled down the crowded street to Club Trigger. Madge is an exuberant dog, but while we were out on dates, her behavior would change. She did not always let the guys pet her, which I adopted as part of my dating screening process. If I felt some type of attraction during the first date, I would take Madge's harness off to see if the guy got her approval. Some men she ignored completely, turning her back to them and placing her head on my lap. Other guys got Madge to stand on her hind legs while she stole kisses from them.

Aside from scoring high on the Madge match test, Nate was a fellow writer, which I found intriguing. He was also Brazilian, even though both his first and last name sounded more German, which allowed me to practice my rusty Portuguese. Nate wanted to go clubbing, which is not the best thing to do with a guide dog. Feeling comfortable with Nate, I left Madge at home with my family. This was only our third date, but it was clear that Nate was picking up the blind etiquette fairly quickly. I complimented his ability to guide me through the crowds in the Castro. He reminded me that he was blind in one eye, making me recall the difficulty of struggling with vision in only one eye.

Brushing up against strangers, we made our way through the packed club. I could tell by the plush sofa, sleek new floor, and acoustics that the venue had been recently remodeled. I folded my cane into my coat pocket. Nate inquired, "So, does that cane have a name too?"

I flashed him a smile before answering, "Yup, they all do. This one is Sugar Cane. I broke Candy Cane last week while packing my bag for the gym." I heard his laughter over the music and felt him clink my beer.

After a round of beers, Nate and I hit the dance floor. Some of the music took me back to my sighted days. I felt a body behind me and quickly turned around to investigate. My forehead bumped softly into a visor, and I heard a deep voice say, "You okay. I won't hurt ya."

I heard Nate say, "He's blind," as he pulled me closer to him. Without my cane or Madge, I was just another dancing body in a loud, dark club. The stranger replied, "Are you serious?! You don't look blind at all." Being used to this type of comment, I simply smiled, pulled out my cane from my pocket, and waved it in the air. The guy apologized, and his voice faded with the song.

Nate grabbed my hand and slowly pulled me back to the sofa. I asked, "Need a break?"

I felt his body sink into the couch while he said, "Yup, I guess I'm too old for ya, eh?"

Not being able to gauge his tone adequately, I assumed he was playing and retorted, "Should I bring you your oxygen mask?" I felt his body tense up next to mine. I realized my comment was not funny to him, and I began to feel bad,

"Forty is not old at all. Besides, that stuff doesn't matter to me."

He responded, "Well, everyone keeps lookin' at you probably tryin' to figure out why you are holding on to me. You can't see it, but that guy who tried to dance with you had been checking you out for a while."

Shrugging my shoulders, I answered, "So?! I'm with you." Nate excused himself to go to the bathroom, and I sunk down on the sofa to wait for him.

I heard the same deep voice from earlier say, "Hey, it's me again." Reminding myself that most people are not familiar with blind etiquette, I replied, "Hi, Me!"

I heard him chuckle in response, and I sat up in my seat. "I'm Anthony," the man shouted over the music. He asked me if Nate was my boyfriend, and I told him we'd only been dating a short time. Anthony inquired, "So, how old do I sound?"

I honestly answered, "I dunno know, fifty?"

I could feel him tense up, and he cleared his throat before replying, "I guess I should stop smoking. I'm 34 but look younger." He took my hand and glided it over his six pack. I sensed a body sit down next to me. Smelling the cologne, I realized it was Nate. Feeling slutty, I looked back at Nate with *sorry, sorry, sorry* eyes and introduced them to each other.

Anthony excused himself, and Nate exclaimed sarcastically, "He's cute! Don't let him get away." I explained to him that muscular bodies feel nice, but at the end of the day, content was way more important. It was weird for me to hear someone feeling insecure about himself while hanging out with me.

I unfolded Sugar Cane and placed her on the sofa. A raspy voice asked, "Where did you get that glow stick?" Nate and I both laughed, and we explained it was a cane and that

I was blind. The stranger's comment helped melt some of the awkwardness between us and we resumed having fun.

Despite the occasional laughing and dancing, Nate continued to highlight his insecurities about his appearance for the rest of the night. His comments reminded me that I lived in a visual-centric world. I had learned a new way to gauge art, beauty, and comfort, yet I was discovering that other people still were limited by their vision.

36

Night Light

One of the first phobias I recall developing was fear of the dark. I would often try to bargain with my parents to let me keep my bedroom light on. Initially, my family was okay with it and would just turn off the lights once I was asleep. However, by the time I was in the first grade, they wanted to break the habit.

My mom's booming botanica business kept both my parents busy and away from home most of the time. My older sisters, like most siblings, preyed on my fear, making me hysterical and unable to sleep. Notes from my teacher stating that I frequently fell asleep in class gave my mom the idea to take me out of school for a few days and talk to me about my nyctophobia.

I was thrilled to miss school and finally get to see where my parents worked. The shop was made up of two equally large rooms. The back room was where my dad spent most of the time on the phone or unpacking items. My mom managed the front and dealt with all the customers. I spent the first couple of hours sniffing oils, candles, and bags with dried plants, while my mom helped the numerous men and women who visited the shop. Later in the afternoon, the crowd died down, and my mom began to ask me questions. "So, are you having nightmares?"

I softly answered in the negative and explained that I hated to be in the dark. I could not put my thoughts into words, but she seemed to understand my choppy answers. She pulled her long red hair away from her face and sat me on the glass countertop next to the cash register. She brought statues to me and began to explain who they were, taking breaks to help customers.

As I learned who each figure was, I paid attention to the people who bought the statues. In the course of a few days, I learned about Shiva, Buddha, Jesus, and what a menorah represented. She told me how darkness is only scary because it's hard to see what is around, but we could all create our own light. Placing her hands over my eyes, she had me imagine the lights she was talking about. I remember seeing white and red lights floating, and I cheered when I realized I could beat the dark.

Being blind combined my adult fear of being alone and my childhood fear of darkness. I have sometimes felt that because I could not see people, they could not see me either. After two years in blindness, I often found the need to psych myself up some mornings before starting the day. I would spend hours in my dorm room, lying in bed, thinking about how only two years prior, I was able to see.

This particular morning, I was suffering from the biggest self-doubt episode I had encountered since the days immediately following the first surgery. I had broken up with Nate a few days earlier and was starting to feel unsure about my decision. I was afraid that I would never find someone else who would run errands, read my mail, or buy Madge toys. However, I also reflected on the numerous jealous outbursts and the controlling behavior that signaled he was not the one for me.

After basking in sorrow and doubt for a while, I reluctantly got up and began to get ready to take the train to San Francisco. I fed and relieved Madge, smiling at how she would do her business on command. Ironically, what I thought would be the toughest part of working with a guide dog was by far to me the easiest aspect of the partnership. I placed my duffel bag on my bed and began to stuff in clothes and toiletries, taking short breaks to enjoy a song on the radio and dance with Madge. I was ready to head down to the Caltrain station, when I reached for my bag and noticed something poking out from the zipper. I dug my fingers past the metal teeth and realized Madge had stuffed her Nylabone in the bag.

Wiping a tear from my cheek, I kneeled down and gave Madge a hug. My fears may never quite go away, but knowing I had a four-legged night-light put me at ease.

37

Capoeirista

Sophie and I started to hang out almost immediately after her arrival at OCB. In just a few days, she made quite an impact on the entire student body. The partially blind men described her as a blind Betty Boop, and the totally blind were charmed by her melodic voice. Most of the men went out of their way to show her around campus, causing competition among the women. Many of the women found her annoying, crude, and felt uncomfortable with her bisexuality. Being young and adventurous automatically made her cool in my mind.

During PE class, we began to talk about growing up in east San Jose. Although I am six years older and attended different schools, we were both raised in the same multiracial community. We laughed as we stretched over mats, reminiscing about growing up with drag queens as friends. I started to do a few Capoeira movements on the floor, and Sophie asked what I was doing. I explained that I was doing a headstand and offered to teach her how to do one. She reminded me about the magnet in her head, and I shyly replied, "Oh my bad," and continued with my Capoeira sequences.

Sophie was only twenty-two but had suffered from some brain disease. One day, she woke up blind and was rushed to the hospital. That visit turned into surgeries in an attempt to save her life. As a result, she ended up with a magnet in her head "to keep the flow in her head normal," as she described it. No matter how many times she explained her situation, I never seemed to grasp what happened completely. What I do know is that it must have been terrifying. Sophie added, "Besides, I have a weave, and I can't mess it up."

I laughed and asked, "Can you see what I am doing now?"

She only could see movement and responded, "Um, I can see something moving back and forth but can't tell what it is." I told her I was doing Capoeira and that I had trained for twelve years. Sophie exclaimed, "Oh my gosh. My friend does Capoeira too!"

Up until then, I figured that I would never be able to train again. Capoeira is highly acrobatic and is done to live music. I figured the drumming and singing would keep me from hearing what was happening, making the rhythmic art no longer available to me. I was not surprised by her answer, because there are so many Capoeira schools in the Bay Area. I sighed before saying, "Oh, that's nice."

I started to walk on my hands, and Sophie continued, "Yeah, she has been doing it for a while. She's blind too." Her comment sent a jolt down my spine. I had two fears holding me back from returning to the art form that taught me confidence, discipline, and how to be playful. My first concern was that people would wonder how it was possible for a Capoeirista to lose a fight. The mere thought made me feel ashamed and unable to face Mestre Vaginho. My second concern was being rejected because of my disability and only allowed to drum.

Sophie's words gave me hope, and I sprang toward her voice, "Really? Who is your friend? Where does she train?"

I was speaking so fast, she had me repeat myself twice to understand me. Her laugh filled the gym, and an instructor asked us to keep quiet. Sophie told me she met C. J. at a blind center in San Jose. They briefly dated but were now good friends. I said, "A blind lesbian Capoeirista! Very cool." Daydreams of training again flooded my mind. This C. J. woman had somehow figured out how to do it all blindly and helped pave the way for me.

Sophie added, "I think C. J.'s real name is Claribel."

I picked up my jaw from the floor and asked, "Are you sure that's her name? I think I know her." I told her about the Claribel who had gone to high school with me and also trained at my academy with Mestre Vaginho. We compared notes and agreed we were both talking about the same person. I could not believe what I was hearing: one of my childhood friends was both gay and blind.

I got Claribel's number from Sophie and called her later that night. We were both in shock and struggled to talk over one another. Claribel said, "This is crazy. I'm going to come see you in the city this weekend."

Claribel and I hit the Castro, and after a few drinks, we got to the touchy subjects. I inquired, "So, how did it happen?" She sighed and told me it was diabetes. Thanks to the practice I got at OCB, I had figured out a way to tell my story that was brief, yet answered everyone's questions. She gave me a hug, and I smiled, feeling her spiky hair on my cheek.

Claribel was now C. J., and it was clear to my fingers we shared the same taste in clothes. I said, "I think I have a shirt just like this one." She started to tell me how annoying it was to get confused for a boy by gay men. I asked, "So, aren't you going to ask how I could let those guys beat me up?"

C. J. said, "Dude, we were never taught to fight friends, and there were more of them. The fact you are alive shows you did somethin' right." She encouraged me to go back to training and explained how Vaginho had developed a technique to train her. "It's not so hard, Belo. Just give it a try."

A few weeks later, I agreed to attend a class with C. J. The entire ride to the academy was filled with thoughts of failure and fear. I knew by now that all blind people are different, and maybe I would not pick up this technique as well as C. J. The cab driver announced our stop, and C. J. dragged me out from the car, "Quick, slow poke, this way."

Vaginho had moved his school from San Jose to Sunnyvale, since I last trained with him. The idea of a new building also made me very nervous. I heard his caring voice and sensed my eyes tear behind my shades. Vaginho called, "Oh man! There are two of you now! That's very cool!" He called C. J. by her Capoiera name, asking "Penguin, is this the surprise you told me about?" C. J. laughed, and my own laugh shortly followed. He gave me a strong hug and said, "Welcome back, Cheiroso! Let's get you guys going here."

C. J. had also done some teaching of her own, and everyone at the academy was well versed in blind etiquette. No one was rude, and all my former classmates were simply happy to see me. The drills were not as difficult as I expected and got even easier throughout the class. That evening, I sweated all the anxiety and self-doubt away and had both faith and hope for my Capoeira future.

Vaginho and the rest of the students were deeply supportive and encouraging. Yet, the distance between Sunnyvale and San Francisco was too great to commit to, and after a few classes, I struggled to get there, after missing the train or not having eighty dollars for the cab fare. Feeling brave, I decided to approach the local schools in San Francisco and was disappointed with their reaction. Some of the groups referred to me as a liability and would only train me through private instruction. At first, it seemed like a possibility, until I was hit with a fifty dollars per session cost. Other schools never returned my phone calls or emails. Even after I would tell them I held a yellow/blue belt, they seemed disinterested in the idea of a blind Capoeirista. Tired of being rejected and reminded of my limitations caused me to put the idea of training Capoeira on the shelf for the time being. A year later, C. J. invited me to the Batizado where she would get her yellow/blue belt. She had caught up to me, and I was happy for her but sad for me.

Norah from OCB had just gotten an apartment in Berkeley, and I decided to take her up on the invitation to come over. Madge, Norah, and I went out to explore her new neighborhood. We weren't too far from her apartment, when I heard that familiar song. We walked toward the music, and I heard the Capoiera games. Norah asked about classes for the blind, and a charismatic voice answered, "Sure, but you should talk to the Mestre first."

I asked, "Who is the master here?"

The stranger replied, "Mestre Accordion."

Ever since I could remember, I knew his name. Mestre Accordion is a living legend in the Capoeira community. I recalled taking a class from him ten years prior at an event in Canada, but I hesitated to get excited after my previous encounters with the other schools. I took the number down and decided to call some other time.

The next day, while packing my bag to head down to the dorms at NDNU, I found my Capoiera uniform in a drawer and decided to call the school in Berkeley. The guy who answered was honest and told me, "It's new territory for us, but we're not scared."

Later that same weekend, I showed up all dressed in white at the school on San Pablo Street. Mestre Accordion was super friendly and excited to work with me. He even had a space set up for Madge to watch me train. He started me off with a few movements on my own to gauge my level and, in a few minutes, had me working with the other students.

The two-hour class was exhausting, but I refused to take any breaks. Fearful of looking weak, I attempted every move being taught, even if I had not tried it without vision before. At the conclusion of the class when we gathered in the *roda*, or circle, to play, Mestre Accordion began a Capoiera game with me. Everyone clapped and cheered as I tried to duck under his kicks and kick back. Playing with him reminded me how fun Capoiera can be, and I released all the anxiety I had been holding for so long. We finished our game, and I returned to the circle to clap and sing where occasionally I was brought back inside the *roda* to play with other students. The games came to an end, and Mestre Accordion announced, "This is Belo, and he plays good Capoiera. He will be training with us now." The clapping and cheering sealed my adoption. I was finally accepted by a school and acknowledged as a blind Capoerista.

38

Room 102

I was approaching the end of my freshmen year at NDNU when I decided that living on campus would keep me more focused on my studies and away from all the distractions at home. Still a capricious teenager, I justified that if I was truly to escape Mom's habit of running every appliance at the same time and my sister's constant loud music and revolving door of friends and visitors, I'd have to move into a single-occupancy dorm room.

During a quiet lunch at the school's cafeteria, my friend Marisa mentioned that there was a single room with a bathroom attached to it open in St. Joe's Hall. I was sure that room was destined to be mine and even joked about moving in by the end of the week.

One housing application and a phone message later, I eagerly awaited some type of response. The reply I was anxious for came in the form of a letter with my new housing arrangements, and it clearly did not mention St. Joseph's Hall in any way. I was to live in the campus apartments with two other strangers and share the upkeep of a common kitchen, bathroom, and living room area. I could feel the blood making its way to my face, giving me the numb effect I passionately hate. I crumpled the piece of paper so furiously that I ended up giving myself one of those annoying paper cuts that go on reminding one of its presence for days.

I wasn't ready to give up without at least trying to get my way somehow. I have never been close to my father and can count with one hand the times he has been there for me. Nevertheless, I figured this was one of those rare moments when asking for his support and advocacy seemed like a good idea. A series of phone calls and emails later, we were granted a meeting with Carrie in the housing office. She was extremely kind and courteous through the initial dialogue. I clearly remember shaking her hand, my paper cut still making itself known. She asked both my father and me to take a seat and went on to inform us that the specific room I had in mind had been intended for students with handicaps and that they had a student already assigned to it. She then explained the Americans with Disabilities Act and how it makes things fair for others. She had tons of information; however, I started to tune her out. My dad didn't say much, but his stare was a thesaurus of words of disapproval toward me. All of a sudden, I felt guilty for feeling so strongly about something that was never really mine to begin with.

The following week, I ended up moving into the living situation assigned to me. A few people at school asked why I never moved to St. Joe's after I had announced to anyone who would listen that the room was mine. The only response I could come up with at that time was, "That's a handicap room, and some cripple is supposed to move in. I guess they need it more, since they have such a horrible life and all."

The mysterious student never showed up, and the room remained empty. I remember walking a friend to her room late one night after watching a scary movie and passing right by that room. I slowly paused and stared at the wooden door, the three metal numbers nailed on the door staring right back. I walked away from the door, mumbling, "Whatever, whatever, whatever."

Years later, after making the decision to go back to school to pursue writing, I decided to return to a familiar place. My blindness sometimes discouraged me from venturing into new horizons, and I often chose to keep things simple. I decided to spend the summer in Belmont to get away from my Mission Street condo. I spoke to Jenna Smalls in housing, who was a pleasure. She said they had the perfect place for me and my guide dog Madge.

It was both scary and exciting to be back in a place where I spent so much time when I had sight. I immediately recognized the steep hill on the main entrance as my sister made her way through the winding campus. Jenna Smalls met up with my family, and we quickly began to make our way to my new room. I heard a set of keys chime and then a squeaky door open. Jenna said, "Here we are; this is St. Joe's 102 ..."

I could feel the tears starting to form and make their way to the surface of my eyes. I excused myself with the plan to take Madge for a quick walk. My sisters, unaware of my history with the room, told me to go ahead. A few moments later, I made my way to a grassy patch to let Madge relieve herself. Making tears is the only thing my eyes are good for, and I was begging them to have mercy, not on me but on my family who has already endured so much. It would kill their souls to see me cry. I promised my eyes some relieving time of their own and made my way back to Room 102.

When I arrived, my sister had unpacked everything for me, and she helped me walk my fingers through my room. As my family made their way out, I felt for the surface of the door. Closing the door behind them, I heard rubber shoes shuffling their way out on the carpet. The door felt nothing like what I know it looked like, it felt smooth and impenetrable. I leaned my back against it and slid down to the floor. My eyes quickly began to collect what was owed, and I let myself feel everything I had been bottling for the last hour. I gingerly caressed my thumb on the side of my hand where a paper cut once lay nearly ten years ago.

39

Back for the First Time

The bells from the school's chapel began to ring and announce the new day. Ever since I lost my sight, I had moved from one dorm to another while acquiring new skills for survival. However, unlike OCB and Guide Dogs, the dorms at NDNU were familiar to me since I had spent years in them while a mischievous teen and hyper early twenty-something. Although I was not crazy about living amongst hormonal young people again, I knew it was much easier to live on campus than commute every day from San Francisco down the Peninsula to Belmont.

The recession was in full swing, and I thought it would be more beneficial to go back to school, instead of trying to work in such a tough job market. Magley, like many companies that serviced the financial sector, was hit really hard by the mortgage meltdown, so I was not surprised when they started to lay people off. Just like after the dot-com bubble burst, each round of layoffs was proceeded by a gloomy vibe that filled the office space. Unlike my coworkers, it didn't bother me to receive the pink slip. I had survived losing my sight, and everything else just seemed small in comparison.

It was relaxing to shed my dress shirt and ties for sweatpants and sandals. Madge also seemed to enjoy the large fields and the other animals that made up the fifty-acre forest campus.

Fortunately, Madge was my only roommate. I had a boyfriend, a guide dog, and thought I was comfortable being blind. Nevertheless, a few weeks into the school year, I started to feel lonely. My boyfriend would say, "They're really young, Belo. They probably don't know how to handle your blindness." With the exception of faculty and staff, most of the residents would not talk to me or join me for a meal at the school's cafeteria. Eating alone soon became a habit, and for the first time in my life, I accepted the fact I would be a loner at this school.

When I was sighted, my loud voice and laughter filled every inch of this hilled and sloped campus. I had friends coming out of my ears and an overscheduled social agenda. I tried to comprehend how I could have no problems mingling in public in San Francisco but struggled to get some type of acknowledgment on the college campus. Perhaps, being gay and blind was too weird for many of the inexperienced young adults to handle. Yet, I hoped that some of the girls would not have an issue and eagerly waited for one of them to reach out.

At times, I would feel restless while hearing people talking about me in the cafeteria, pretending I was not there: "How do you think he dresses himself?" or "Do you think the dog sleeps with him?" I began to feel like a foreigner who people did not know how to treat or understand. My PDA became my weapon against isolation.

Although my classmates in the graduate program were very social and inclusive toward me, none of them lived on campus, making me dread the day and anxiously await the evening seminars where I would finally be addressed like a person.

I soon became irritated with myself, because I knew that the younger social version of me was a result of my own desire to reach out to others. One of my teachers in junior high once told me, "I would give you a time-out and send you to the corner, but then you would just talk to the wall." Now, my blindness kept me from reaching out to others. Attempting to socialize, I found myself once or twice talking to an empty seat or thin air. Embarrassed when someone would point out the awkward moment, I decided to give up on making friends and rationalized that I had plenty of them in the real world.

It took some time, but, like many outsiders, I was eventually brought back into society by an unexpected group of people. It was not the theater or English majors with their outgoing personalities who first talked to me but the athletes. The lacrosse and soccer teams would sometimes all sit with me and help me get items from the food bar. Members of the basketball team soon followed, and I was shocked to have all these manly men comfortable taking my hand to help me navigate chairs and tables or even pick up after me. Other students soon followed, and I slowly started to have guests at my table. Leah, a budding actress, became a regular meal buddy and helped me memorize names.

Some people believe that pictures are worth a thousand words, but I believe that sounds create worlds just as vividly. I think that many sighted people are misled by stereotypes of the blind that are outdated because of technology or are untrue because they were crafted by sighted people. We use the phrase "I see" to establish our understanding of a thought or idea. However, if a person does not physically see, it could be interpreted as not understanding the world. The athletes who took a first leap to befriend me were able to not only see, but hear me.

40

Blind Again

As I reclaimed my life by learning to do everything the blind way, my desire for justice and revenge weakened. Two long years had passed, and, at times, I felt like my civil lawsuit was the only thing keeping me from moving forward. The constant questioning from family, coworkers, and classmates regarding my legal case often made me feel neglectful, since I no longer shared their outrage. When my attorney finally called with a mediation date, I treated it like an errand that was dreaded but essential, like a trip to the DMV.

Elizabeth, my attorney, picked me up and went over the process of mediation. "Don't worry, Belo. Jason and I will both fight hard for you," she said while battling through downtown traffic.

We met up with Jason at the entrance of the mediation offices and were quickly ushered into a small conference room. Jason spotted the Lopez brothers and their accomplices and began to narrate the scene for me. "I see them all here, Belo. Looks like they have a legal team with them."

I felt like a piece of furniture, unable to see or talk, just a lifeless artifact in the room, without a thought or voice. Pictures of the assault fluttered into my mind. I began to feel anxious as Carlos spoke at a distance, probably in the hallway. It was the first time I had heard that voice since the night of my assault, and my stomach flipped. Elizabeth must have noticed my discomfort because she got up from her chair to close the door to the small room without saying anything to me. She handed me a cup of water and began to go over my medical files, reliving the torture of gaining and losing sight. Over a matter of minutes, I reexperienced the months of seeing blurry snapshots, shadows and movement, and eventually having total darkness. Each experience with sight was brief, eventually leaving me blind again.

I heard a man come in and introduce himself as the judge overseeing the mediation process. He tapped my shoulder and said, "Don't worry, Mr. Cipriani; we should be done before lunch time."

He then told my lawyers he thought this would be a breeze and looked forward to a long Italian meal. The brothers and attorneys were seated in another room, and the judge stepped out to meet them as well.

Hearing the judge's heavy footsteps running back and forth between conference rooms became the routine throughout the day. Elizabeth, as she promised, argued and fought like a true warrior, leaving little to no room for questions.

We took a late lunch break, and the judge said he was disappointed that an agreement had not been reached. I had not said a word for hours, and when I began to talk over my tuna melt, my voice sounded rough and weak. "So, how do you think it's going?" I asked. Elizabeth and Jason both said that the judge seemed reasonable, but that it was too early to tell.

When we got back to the mediation office, the judge's dance between rooms continued for a few more hours. Again, I did not say anything and thought back to all the words of wisdom spoken by my mom and Mestre Vaginho. I was poised and pretended to be unfazed by a group of people discussing and analyzing my life with a fine-tooth comb.

We all finally agreed on a ridiculous and depressing sum of money and adjourned the mediation. The figure was less than what I used to make per year as an inexperienced recruiter. Both Elizabeth and Jason apologized.

"You won, but you are not being compensated correctly," Elizabeth said, as we drove back to my home. She walked me to my door and gave me a big hug. I arrived at a quiet apartment and headed straight to my room. I could hear my sister in her bedroom, and Madge ran out to find me. I locked myself and Madge in my room. I took my tie off and jumped in bed, sobbing. Reflecting on the day's events, I called Madge onto the bed, and for the first time, she hesitated. We both knew it was against the rules, but after a few seconds, she sprang up and began to lick my tears. I held on tight to her soft body, thinking how justice was blind—again.

41

Teeth

It had been a while in which I had spent so much time on my back. My mouth was beginning to get sore, but I refused to complain. I wanted my dental student to concentrate and complete the exam. The drilling device stopped, and he squeezed my hand before calling one of the instructors over. A perky woman sat really close to me and said, "What a cute dog! Are you a trainer?"

I shook my head and answered, "Nope, I'm blind." Just like strangers often do, she apologized for my blindness as if it were her fault.

In the initial phase of my blindhood, comments like these would anger me. Nevertheless, through the passage of time, I learned that it is a person's own discomfort with blind people that makes them act nervous and say dumb things. Today, however, was not about me but about him. I resumed my role as a student-patient and allowed the woman to examine my teeth, ignoring all the silly and borderline ridiculous questions that came from her mouth. The assessment came to an end, and I followed Madge out to the lobby. The dental student took a seat next to me and tapped his feet anxiously on the hard floor. I said, "You did fine. Chillax!"

He laughed and held my hand, proudly introducing

Madge and me to his instructors and classmates. A woman called his name from the neighboring room, and he jumped out of his chair to fetch his results. I was focused so hard on visualizing him passing the exam that I was slightly startled when an older woman on my left said, "Hello, it's me."

We had spent nearly five hours at this student clinic, and I figured because she had seen me for all that time, she assumed I would recognize her. I greeted the older voice politely, placing my hand over Madge's head. Many strangers often want to feed or pet Madge, making me wary around people I do not know, who may be unfamiliar with guide dog etiquette. The lady continued, "Is that your boyfriend?" I remember we were outside the city limits, and I mentally prepared myself for a homophobic comment. I told her we had been together for a few months and that I was very happy. She proceeded to inquire, "That's nice, but do you know he's black? I mean, you look so sweet and nice."

I had been with Jim for years and never encountered any racist comments. However, that's the thing about blindness; it makes people feel free to say things they might not normally say.

Stunned, I stayed quiet and inwardly sighed when I heard him running back toward me. "Babe, I passed! I got 100 percent, and it's all thanks to you!"

Mom once told me you know when you're falling for someone; you begin to act in order to make them happy. My performance began with clapping and cheering and led to hugging. Even Madge joined in when I took her harness off. She hopped all over the place, giving us both plenty of kisses, pressing her teeth against both cheeks. The comment still burned, but I pushed it aside, wanting to be a good boyfriend and keep the vibe positive. I could thank my blindness for simplifying the process of ignoring people and focusing on what is most valuable. "Let's celebrate and go get a good dinner," I said, flashing my newly polished teeth for all to see.

42

Baby Braille

As a blind man, I often feel like I am on display in the sighted world. I'm a part of the daily life of many San Franciscans whose names I will never learn. They greet me on the BART and while Madge and I zip through crowds in the Castro and Mission districts. Their "hellos" are often warm and drenched in awe and admiration while Madge and I conquer the city's intersections. Because I can sense people's stares prickle the nape of my neck, I feel as if I have no privacy. Something that allows me to take some privacy back is increasing the tempo on the electronics voices from my devices to the point where it sounds like gibberish to most people. I text away while waiting for the bus or listen to a book at a coffee shop, feeling relieved that no one really knows what I am doing.

I was listening to a text message, while Madge led me to a seat in a neighborhood café, when I heard a young woman say on my right, "Welcome back, soy latté and a sesame bagel, right?"

I had only stopped at this coffee shop once a few weeks ago, yet the woman remembered my order. I smiled and responded, as I finished typing a text message to my boyfriend, "Yes, that's exactly it."

The girl asked curiously, "That's so fast; is it Japanese?"

I flashed her a smile before answering, "Nope, it's English."

She patted my shoulder, and I heard her shoes tap the linoleum floor and fade into a chorus of voices and rattling plates. I slipped Madge a piece of kibble and told her, "You're so popular; they remember me cuz of you." She licked my palm and laid her head on my shoe. I enjoyed my food and worked on some homework.

I was about to complete my first semester of grad school, and I still found it strange that I was doing better as a blind student than when I was sighted. "Too many visual distractions," I said to myself as I let the warm bread and cheese melt in my mouth. I also supposed it makes it easier to focus when one is studying what interests him. I had always wanted to be a writer, yet it was not until I lost my sight that I pursued it seriously. It was incredibly rewarding and fulfilling when my instructors and peers began to notice and compliment my work. I had slowly begun to fill the spaces in myself that had been emptied.

I finished my breakfast and thought about the next item on my agenda. I always had an interest in fashion and style. Once I learned to buy clothes online and style my hair into any 'do, I fell back into familiar shopping and grooming patterns. One of these patterns was a biweekly trip to Hair Studio. "Madge, let's go get my hair cut."

I left a few bills on the small round table and followed Madge out the door and into the street.

Rafael greeted me with a warm, "Hi, Belo; have a seat. I'll be right with you."

The salon seemed quiet for a Friday, and I took a seat and pulled out my Braille PDA. I felt a small hand on my shoulder and heard a woman say, "Hi, sorry to bother you, but can I ask you a question?"

I figured she was about to inquire about Madge or perhaps wanted to know if I had any vision and braced myself for either. The woman continued, "Um, my grandson was born blind and, um, my daughter is really young. I guess what I'm trying to ask is if you know what we should do?"

In all my training at the LightHouse, OCB and Guide Dogs for the Blind, this question never arose. I felt my throat contract as I realized how important anything I would say to this woman would be for her. I thought about all the blind women I met who raised healthy sighted and blind children and said, "There is a blind baby foundation, and I'm sure that is the best place to start. I would call the LightHouse for the Blind as well."

The woman continued to tell me about how smart she knew her grandson was. "Every time I talk to him, he looks my way." Her biggest concern was that the family wouldn't know how to provide the right support. "I'm Carla, by the way," she said.

Thinking for a moment, I continued, "I don't think anyone is born with the ability to raise a blind child. What I have seen, though, are many people who are born blind who are afraid of the world. There is nothing wrong with letting him bump into furniture and get dirty. It is how he'll learn. Also, if his mobility is good, he could get a guide dog at sixteen. It's the driving age, you know."

Carla's laughter made me feel grateful that through fate I had met people who directed me in my journey into blindness. I mentally thanked and acknowledged my social workers, mentors, and rehab counselor who gave me the tools to become a competent blind person. I told Carla, "It's hard sometimes, but it also keeps life interesting. I'm working for a consulting firm downtown, working on my master's, and I practice martial arts. I even have a boyfriend who is sighted and lets me be independent."

I could feel Carla begin to relax and she asked, "Do they have baby Braille or something like that?"

I paused for a second before answering, "I don't think so, but they've got all these cool talking gadgets. Let me show you."

I did not have all the answers for Carla, and I might never know everything there is to know about blindness. However, since 2007, I've picked up the skills that will allow me to survive and enjoy a truly unique life. It took an unfamiliar voice to confirm that my transformation was complete. Madge and I left the salon where I was embraced by the San Francisco breeze that caressed my hair and reaffirmed my rebirth.